Bless This Mess

Joanna Campbell-Slan

Dedicated to:
Chris Blair, Carolanne Zink, Terry Bartels,
and Bonnie Kaufman for the good that they see in others.

Acknowledgements. Thanks to the sales team at F&W Publications for their support of this book. Thank you to Matt Piskulic of VIP Graphics, St. Louis, MO, for the cover and interior design.

Limit of Liability & Disclaimer. The author and publisher have used their best efforts in preparing this book. The author and publisher make no warranty of any kind, expressed or implied, with regard to the instructions and suggestions contained in this book.

Bless This Mess: Motivation for Moms through stories that inspire & uplift.

First Edition. Printed and bound in the United States of America.

05   04   03   02   01   5   4   3   2   1

Library of Congress Catalog Card Number: 2001096334
ISBN: 1-930500-06-8

Published by:
EFG, Inc. • St. Louis, MO• www.scrapbookstorytelling.com

Distributed to the trade by:
Writer's Digest Books
An imprint of F&W Publications
1507 Dana Ave., Cincinnati, OH 45207
(800) 289-0963; fax: (513) 531-4082

Contents

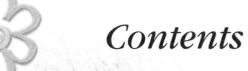

Bless This Mess!

Contents

Contents

Welcome

When Mama's Happy, Everybody's Happy

Linda's kitchen holds many happy memories for me. Before I was a mom, I'd marvel at her son playing with toys spread all over the kitchen floor as Linda cooked close by, cheerfully unaware of the mess. After I had my son, Michael, I appreciated her wisdom even more.

It was my friend Linda who peeked into Michael's poopy diaper and pronounced it "just right" for a breast-fed baby, after I had worried myself sick and driven the pediatrician crazy with concern that the baby had diarrhea.

It was Linda who always reminded me of the bigger plan of life, even when everything was changing rapidly and I wondered if I'd ever achieve any of my career goals. And, it was Linda who startled me with her sweatshirt slogan, "If Mama Ain't Happy, Ain't Nobody Happy."

Several years after seeing Linda's sweatshirt, I was reminded of the slogan. We were eating at Red Lobster when my husband, son and I found ourselves mesmerized by the loud voice of an angry woman at the next table.

"I do everything around the house, and everything for this family. I'm sick of it. I'm not going to quit my job because we need the money. What I need is help and cooperation from

Welcome

all of you," she swallowed a chunk of lobster and pointed from child to child and then to her husband. "That includes you, and you and you."

Lisa, you could help with the cooking." Then the mother turned to her husband, "And you could get up off your behind and pitch in once in a while, too."

By the end of her tirade, the entire restaurant had hushed to listen. As if we were the audience in a play, we sat stunned by the performance. "Boy, is she mad," whispered my son.

It's not easy to bring home the bacon, fry it up in a pan and then do the dishes as well. This poor woman was at the end of her proverbial rope. Haven't we all been there at one time or another? When a woman is so overwrought, the entire family suffers from heart disease.

Like it or not, women are the heart of the home. Only when Mama's happy can the rest of the family be happy.

This book is for you. It's filled with ideas to find the blessings within the messes of being a mom. It's also designed to help you take care of yourself so that you have the heart to take care of the rest of your family.

Blessings to you and yours,

Joanna

Hectic Households

Hectic Households

Mom Advice

From the moment you start to "show" that you are pregnant, you become a magnet for advice, much of which will be unwanted and unwarranted. You'll find your own way of coping with that nonsense. You can nod sagely and walk away. You can pull an Ann Landers and ask, "Why would this be your concern?" You can muffle your screams and sob later in the bathroom. But don't, under any circumstances, let the bad advice keep you from picking up a few gems here and there.

The best advice is Mom advice; advice that is tested and tried by another mother. Mom advice isn't packaged by expensive marketing firms, so it's easy to miss. Mom advice doesn't usually come from the loudmouths who tell you what to do. Moms usually casually mention a tip that worked for them. Often they share the tip in an apologetic manner because Moms have tested these ideas under fire, and we do not have any official body backing up our claims.

Here are a few of my favorites:

1. **Throw away the shoes**. (Don't be afraid to make rules and stick to them.) Margaret worries about her youngest daughter and young visitors swallowing Barbie shoes, so the rule in Meg's house is "hand over the shoes." When a new outfit is

Hectic Households

purchased, the footwear goes immediately to the trash can. More importantly, this behavior is a predictable habit. When you turn a request into a habit, kids may fight you at the git-go, but if you stick to your guns, they become inured.

2. **Save fast food toys and other freebies for a rainy day**. Put them where the kids can't find them and dole them out as needed. Keep special treats and frozen pizzas in the freezer for the same reason. Plan for the bad days, 'cause they will happen.

3. **Pass out a roll of quarters before a long trip**. Levy a fine on riders who fight. This worked for Vickie Heid, and when she shared this with a group of mothers, we immediately saw the wisdom. I've tried the reverse: "You behave and you get XYZ." That didn't work at all! Holding money and then giving it away hurts. You can also downgrade the coins to nickels or dimes as your budget or kids' ages allow.

4. **Never awaken a sleeping kid.** This one has had mixed results for me, but generally if your child falls asleep in the afternoon, I'd say don't wake him or her. Forget about the tooth brushing routine. Let 'em sleep.

5. **Visit the arcade in London, Paris, and so on**. An indignant father roared to me, "I didn't take him all the way to Madrid to play in a stupid arcade. We went to see the culture." Right, well, most kids can handle only so much culture in a day. An hour at the arcade can translate into three hours of good behavior at the museum. Not a bad trade in my book.

Hectic Households

6. **Check it out before you make a judgment**. When Michael couldn't sleep in our new house, all the parenting experts suggested letting him cry himself to Sandman Land. Instead, I curled up along side him. In the middle of the night, I awakened to a terrible racket and he awakened screaming. Seems that the hot air vent was improperly installed and when the temperature dropped and the furnace came on, the vent snapped, crackled and popped. Since this was mid-October, Michael had Halloween on the brain. To him the noise sounded like witches. Needless to say, one quick visit from the contractor and the problem was fixed. This situation taught me to listen before I jumped to conclusions.

7. **Invite other parents to come in and visit when they drop off their kids**. We all have errands to do but taking the time to get to know each other pays enormous dividends. You'll learn whose values are like yours and whom you want to know better. Extra bonus: You'll understand their children better so you can coach your child in the fine art of friendship.

8. **Invest in a sleeping bag**. Once a child has a sleeping bag, he or she can sleep on the floor anywhere, including Mom and Dad's room, when major insecurity strikes. When you have company or when they want to go on overnights, the sleeping bag goes along to make the experience much more homey.

9. **Ask before you buy a gift**. Okay, your kid loves Legos, but maybe the birthday child hates them. Or you think a squirt gun

Hectic Households

is fine, but the other family has made a rule that there will be no guns, period. Ask first and earn undying appreciation from other parents.

10. **Limit your kitchen clean up time**. If your household is like mine, I could live in the kitchen, cooking and cleaning up. That's bad. First, it teaches boys and girls that women belong in the kitchen. Second, it makes nibbling too easy. Set a timer and then scram. The dishes will wait.

11. **Set a timer**. An easy-to-operate kitchen timer is possibly the best discipline investment you'll ever make. Work with your child to decide when she'll get off the phone or when he'll quit watching television, set the timer and then back off. Now the "bad guy" is the timer, not you. Plus, you've taught your child how to allocate time.

12. **For toddler parents**:

❑ Always tuck wipes, an extra diaper and a snack in your purse and in your glove compartment. If you are flying, don't forget a change of clothes for you. If your child upchucks, chances are you'll be in the line of fire.

❑ A variety of cereals presented individually in a muffin pan makes for great entertainment while you cook dinner.

❑ You can add food coloring to bath water or to bubble bath to make personal hygiene more fun. The food coloring doesn't stain the child or the tub. For the bubble bath, add it as the bubbles form.

Hectic Households

❑ It's okay that your child likes your pots, pans, Tupperware and boxes better than her toys. In fact, it's normal. Put away the toys she finds uninteresting and unearth them on a rainy day.

❑ Soft clothes are best. Hand-me-downs are divine.

❑ Your tape player in your car is your best friend. You'll get sick of the songs, but your little ones will sing along for hours.

❑ On an airplane, keep a lollipop for your child for sucking on during take off and touch down. (A sour one will keep your kid swallowing.) We've whiled away airline delays by playing with an inflated balloon (if your child is old enough). When the balloon bounces out of your hands, you'll be amazed at how your fellow adult travelers will gleefully respond by tossing the balloon back.

Hectic Households

BLESSING

I appreciate my problem-solving ability. Give me the patience to look for solutions rather than wasting my energy getting upset.

1) Write down a parenting problem you keep stumbling over.

_____
_____
_____
_____

2) Make a list of your resources. Who might have handled this problem successfully?

_____
_____
_____
_____

3) Brainstorm your problem. Come up with wild and crazy ways to handle it.

_____
_____
_____
_____
_____

4) Commit to trying at least one new solution.

The Well-Run Household

A women's health center in Illinois sponsored the first program I ever attended on balancing your life. At the time, Michael was three months old, I had been self-employed for two years, and my husband David was running several music stores.

The woman teaching the class was a friend, but by the time the evening was over, I wanted to strangle her. Still, it's worth a laugh to ponder her suggestions:

1. Make a list of all your responsibilities. Sit down with your spouse and divide them up equally.

If I had enough time to list and divide up our responsibilities, I wouldn't be worried about balance! Truth is, the way priorities must shift on a dime, rigidly assigning chores simply won't work. Both spouses must be willing to chip in at any given time. When our spouse doesn't recognize the need to help out, we must ask for or hire help.

2. Note those responsibilities you would be glad to delegate and then give them away.

Right. Like *he* has time. Better yet, go through that fabulous list and cross out half the items. Do the socks really need to be matched before they make it into the drawer? Will the domestic

Hectic Households

police arrest us if we don't make our beds? If the carpet isn't vacuumed daily, and we have to replace it sooner because of wear and tear, won't we at least be able to upgrade from the ugly green shag? Face it, your to-do list belongs on the fiction list in the library.

3. Divide up the child care responsibilities.

Easy for her to say. Her son spent every other weekend with his stepmother!

Kids don't slice down the middle like a pecan pie. One night only Mom will do. The next night Daddy is parent numero uno. At our house, we specialize in tag team parenting. The person least likely to blow gets called into the ring. The person with spittle forming at the sides of the mouth steps out.

In the absence of another consenting adult, parents call time-out and explain that bodily injury may follow if the small person does not play quietly in the nursery until the buzzer rings.

4. Plan meals in advance.

We do this. We always use our turn signals before exiting off the highway into the McDonald's parking lot.

5. Do all the laundry at one time so you start the week with everything neat and clean.

Hectic Households

To do all our laundry at once, we'd have to be forced to go to the laundromat. Clean laundry is not a destination, but a never-ending journey at our house.

Once in a while, we decide to clean all our apparel, all at once. To do this, we go naked while the clothes are washing. The rule is: No wearing undies until all the clean knickers are put away. "Put away" is a euphemism for "the laundry basket is sitting inside your bedroom."

6. Do your gift buying all at once for a year in advance.

Huh?

Try this instead: He buys for his family and you buy for yours. David's family went giftless for a while, but I saved myself enormous amounts of stress. The first year, nothing I bought was right. And now, if I show up with the smallest token, David is eternally grateful for my foresight!

7. Carve out time for yourself. Indulge. Soak in the tub. Read a book.

Michael uses the huge tub in our bedroom on a bi-weekly basis. I, on the other hand, do not even have time to wait for it to fill.

I prefer to sit and sob on the floor of the shower. That's a tension reliever my friend forgot to mention: The good old-fashioned cry. Next to a beer, it's as good as it gets.

Hectic Households

Oh, I suppose I did learn a few tips from the session on balance. I learned to put extra garbage bags in the bottom of the trash containers so they will always be handy.

Needless, to say, I walked away from that session feeling disappointed. So, now is my chance to tell you about balance as I see it.

On occasion, the best one can hope for is survival. When that happens, grit your teeth, count your blessings, and go to sleep as early as you can. Life is unpredictable.

Organizing and planning will help, but in the long run, flexibility and a good sense of humor are the only real indispensables. And by the way, if you are dressed, working and your family is healthy, Congratulations! You are doing a terrific job.

Hectic Households

BLESSING

I have so much to be grateful for.
Thank you for giving me the gift of life.

1) *Try taking a few minutes when you first wake up to just be.*
Write down a few things you feel grateful for in the new day.

_____

_____

_____

_____

2) *Write down how this colors the rest of your day.*

_____

_____

_____

_____

3) *Write down one thing you can be grateful for in a difficult*
situation you are facing. How does this change the way you
approach the problem?

_____

_____

_____

_____

Hectic Households

Get Wise: Margaretize

On a small back street in Stuart, Florida, stands my sister Margaret's house. Ask anyone who knows her—Margaret is remarkable.

When tropical storms flooded the intercoastal waterways around the grade school where she teaches, it was Margaret who stayed behind until all the children were either with their parents or safe for the night.

Stubborn to the last, when the water reached crotch-high, it was Margaret who linked arms with my mother and my ten-year-old niece to wade through the raging storm water and make the two-block journey home safely to her own nine-month-old daughter.

Yes, my little sister sports a set of virtues that would make even William Bennett envious.

But of all her talents—and I haven't even touched on her artistic ability or her creativity—the one I envy most is Margaret's talent for organization.

After knowing her for thirty-two years, I have discerned portions of Margaret's secrets. At the risk of keeping her from a career as a professional organizer, I will share them with you:

Hectic Households

1. **Be ruthless**. Toss, toss, toss out and then toss out again half of what is left. Doesn't matter that this bowl came from Great Aunt Jemima. Doesn't matter that these two glasses were wedding gifts. If they aren't useful today, they're in the way.

2. **Group like items**. All electric equipment goes in one box. All craft materials in another place. But—if the item is not more that half full, or worth saving, revert to Rule 1.

3. **Label containers**. Not on the top, where you will never see the words, but on all sides, so no matter how the plastic box is put back on the shelf, you can read what is inside.

4. **Find a place for everything** and keep everything in its place. Pretty stuff can stay on the counter tops. You only need one set of nail clippers if you always put them back where they belong. Cereal goes in the plastic pouring containers so the bugs don't get in. Dog biscuits have their own Tupperware jar, marked, "Bear's biscuits." Oddball items are limited to one junk drawer in the kitchen.

5. **Store seasonal items in the back of closets**. Put what you use daily up front.

6. **Replace old magazine issues** with new ones. Don't keep entire publications. Rip and file—but only if you are truly convinced you will need the clipping you save.

7. **Update important phone numbers** and addresses and post them attractively by the phone. Why dig through scraps of paper?

Hectic Households

8. **Think convenience**. Keep a pen and paper by the phone. Put a place mat under the pet's dishes. Get a plastic holder for your shower goodies.

Before Margaret's daughter was born, Margaret washed, ironed and arranged by size all the baby clothes she had. Watching all this industry made me a little crazy.

"Meg, do you really think you can keep this up after the baby arrives?"

She gave the closet one last admiring glance. "Jonie, this keeps me sane. I can't stand the stress of a mess. I know it will be difficult, but I feel better when I am organized. It's like I'm in control, see?"

She has a point. When there's so little we can control, having a home base that's predictable matters a lot.

After each visit to see Margaret, David and I find ourselves working to streamline our lives. This fall, with Michael's help and permission, we filled two three-foot-tall boxes with old toys and took them to the Salvation Army. For the next three weeks, Michael talked about how happy other children would be to have the toys he no longer enjoyed. Now, he plays more frequently in his room because he can easily find his favorite toys.

Hectic Households

If you don't have the personal strength to begin your program of Margaretizing with a toss and trash session, ask yourself these questions:

1. Would I buy this again today?

2. What do I gain by holding onto this item?

Because I love clothes and have a tough time disposing of old garments, I visualize myself when I was much younger, when I shopped at re-sale shops. I think how much I would have enjoyed buying the clothes I can now afford to give away. Then I let go.

Remember: When the things we own start to own us, it's time to get back in charge.

Hectic Households

BLESSING

I am blessed with abundance in my life. I have enough. It is okay to simplify.

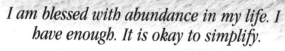

1) Take stock of things you have in your home that irritate you when you see them. What could you do to organize the mess and pare it down?

_____

_____

_____

_____

2) Write down situations to simplify that would have an impact on your mental clutter.

_____

_____

_____

_____

_____

3) What could you do to simplify and uplift your relationships?

_____

_____

_____

_____

Hectic Households

Tackle The Fleas

Denis Waitley once said, "Elephants don't bite, but fleas do." Now, I'm not talking about insects here. I'm thinking about those niggling little loose ends that get under our skin and bother us.

For instance, I must own 200 audio tapes. My car functions as a roving stereo system where I listen to my favorite singers and speakers. I have tapes to inspire, educate and uplift. Unfortunately, they aren't in any order. Trying to find a specific topic or person becomes a project.

One night I sat down and began to number all the tapes. As I numbered them, I listed the topic and person on a sheet of paper. Then I took all the outside plastic cases off. (I once drove off a four-lane highway into the ditch trying to get a tape out of the stupid case. On another occasion, my son closed a case on his mouth and pinched his lip between the top and bottom of the case. He screamed from his car seat in the back seat as I swerved while driving with one hand and trying to disengage his face with the other.)

Finally, I labelled the outside of the plastic shoebox with the numbers of the tapes inside.

Hectic Households

Presto. I felt great.

Okay, sounds trivial to you. But isn't there a similar situation in your life that irritates you? Recipes you'll never use? Old shoes that collect dust? A zillion plastic cups from gas stations? A lump of postal stamps that has glued itself into a paper weight?

Whip those pesky ailments into line. You'll have one less thing to bug you when you exterminate your fleas.

Hectic Households

BLESSING

*I can be the master of my world.
I do have the power to control certain
things. Thank you for giving me the
option to make my life easier.*

1) What has seriously "bugged" you in the past 24 hours?

_____

_____

_____

_____

2) What mess or messes do you contend with on a daily basis?

_____

_____

_____

_____

3) Brainstorm creative ways to circumvent the problem.

_____

_____

_____

_____

*4) Commit to the mess you'll tackle in the future. Give it a
deadline.*

_____

_____

Hectic Households

Too Much
Mrs. Nice Guy

For two weeks straight, I was the P.O.D. That's Slan-speak for Parent On Duty, or married person masquerading as single parent with child. Make that children, since Joon Ho had come to live with us from Korea. One roof, two eleven-year-old boys, and more pre-pubescent hormones than you could shake a stick at—that was life as I knew it.

My dentist once said of his pre-teen boys, "They sound like they are coming right through the ceiling." Right-o. I had never witnessed what they did to make that noise, but the light fixtures shook and shivered. Were they hurling themselves off the tallest dressers in the room? Were they scaling the walls and then pouncing down like over-grown cats? What were they doing? And... did I really want to know?

Growing up in a family of girls, I was caught unaware by the velocity of boydom. So when David, my husband, worked 16-hour days, I found myself whimpering and chanting, "I CAN handle this. I CAN handle this." Part of parenting boys involves pleas for life-saving behaviors: "No, you can't roller blade without a helmet. No, you can't race your scooter down the hill behind the house into the trees. No, the ice on the pond is NOT thick enough for you to walk on." This is balanced, in part, by refueling stops: "Yes, I'm making two pizzas right now. Yes, you can finish all the cookies because if you don't they'll

Hectic Households

be two hours old and probably stale. Yes, I will make macaroni and cheese and mashed potatoes and two burgers for each of you. Now, what would you like for dinner?"

So, one particular morning, when David checked his date book, I was trying to be nice. "I forgot that I have to visit a customer at his house," David looked shame-faced, "and I made an appointment with the plumber, too. Will you be here all morning?"

I took a Lamaze breath while packing two lunch bags. The boys' noontime meals didn't fit inside the lunch bags, so I had to repack or the chow would scatter all the way to their lockers. That morning was my yoga class. I could bypass it. I missed the last class because both Joon Ho and Michael had friends over to spend the night. David was out the door going to work before all four pre-teens awakened. Unfortunately for me, all the kids' parents skipped town. ("I don't remember where my parents went or when they might be home, Mrs. Slan," said one earnest angel. "Could I eat those Doritos with my breakfast?") I reminded myself of all the times I had taken my sweet time retrieving Michael. Turnabout is fair play, but as I broke up a fist fight and phoned in an order for $40 worth of Chinese food, I did feel a little sorry for myself.

"Sorry," David broke into my reverie. "I guess I forgot to check my calendar. Can you handle this?"

Hectic Households

I said, " Yes." Then I started to brood. The truth was I couldn't handle it. Actually, I had reached my limit. The bile was rising in my throat.

Working at home has its good points, but the constant assumption of availability of the person at home creates a situation ripe for distress. I would never presume to schedule David's time, but he occasionally presumes to schedule mine. Then I realized, this could only happen with my permission.

"I'm sorry," I said looking at my husband. "I misspoke. I can't handle it. I really can't handle much more."

David handled the situation with grace. He phoned the plumber and discovered that he had written down the wrong time for the appointment after all. There was never any need for me to give up my class or my scheduled work. And suddenly, I felt great.

Hectic Households

BLESSING

Everything happens for the best. I can speak up for myself and still be nice to others.

1) Are there re-occuring situations where you are too likely to say, "Yes," when you should say, "No"?

_____

_____

_____

_____

_____

2) What do these re-occuring situations say about the way you think of yourself? (For example, I WANT to be a good wife and mother so I find myself saying, "Yes," when I really should be asking for help. Therefore, I have somehow decided that asking for help is NOT a quality of a good wife and mother.)

_____

_____

_____

_____

_____

_____

Hectic Households

3) Is there a particular person who encourages you to overload your schedule? How does this happen and why?

_____

_____

_____

_____

_____

4) Practice saying, "No," in a clear and firm manner—without anger. Write down phrases you might use.

_____

_____

_____

_____

_____

5) When you take on more than you realistically can do, you often hurt people who are uninvolved. Write about an instance where you wound up "punishing" an innocent party by saying, "Yes."

_____

_____

_____

_____

_____

Entertaining Guests

Entertaining Guests

A Guest is a Gift

An old Persian proverb says, "A guest is a gift from God. It is more blessed to feed a stranger than it is to pray all day long."

Donna told us about the proverb as we covered Stephanie's vacuum cleaner case in an old white dresser scarf she had found at a garage sale for 50 cents. A candle in a holder formed the centerpiece. The Thursday night menu never varied: Persian spaghetti, salad with Good Seasons Italian dressing, and a bottle of wine. Whether they really ate spaghetti in Iran was a moot point. By browning a scant quarter of a pound of ground beef with onions, adding nutmeg, cinnamon and enough tumeric to turn the mixture orange, and then plopping in a can of tomato paste, we could coat enough pasta to each have two helpings and leftovers. The money saved on meat went for the wine.

Since then, I've eaten many meals more elaborate and certainly more expensive. But, the best meals have always been those made with love and eaten in good company. We never focused those evenings on what was missing. We took great joy in what we had.

Occasionally, we loose our focus when we have guests. We fuss, we worry, and visions of Martha Stewart make us feel

Entertaining Guests

inadequate. We worry about our cooking, our decor, and our home. We focus on all the wrong things, as we bend over our recipe books. We forget that each voice at the table adds a new seasoning. It is over food that our defenses drop and we become so basic that we can really get to know each other.

Several weeks ago, a valued colleague came to town. My friend Elaine and I worried over the meal we'd promised to prepare. We agonized over the en famille way we both live. Would our guest feel comfortable with children darting in and out? Was it right to mix business and family? The answer came as he spotted Elaine's adorable daughter, two-year-old Daniele. Seeing him with Daniele, he was a different person from the stiff, driven person we had known. This father of two girls (now grown) melted.

We set the prettiest table we could and served our delicious fare: steaks, glazed carrots, mashed potatoes, salad and lemon meringue pie. The meal was wonderful, and a real friendship, one based on mutual values of family and relationships replaced the superficial one we had started.

Entertaining Guests

BLESSING

*It is a gift from God to share what I
have with others. A meal, however
humble, made with affection and
served with joy, is a feast. When we break
bread together, our differences melt away.*

1) *Invite someone you'd like to know better over for dinner, lunch,
tea or breakfast. Whom will you invite?*

_____

_____

_____

_____

_____

_____

2) *Choose something simple to prepare but prepare and serve it
with joy. Set the table with pretty china. Add a flower or a candle.
Note how your relationship evolves after this event.*

_____

_____

_____

_____

_____

_____

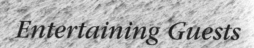

Home for the Holidays

Snow. Snow for Christmas. When the flakes started falling that Friday afternoon, work at the newspaper was suspended. One by one, we advertising salespeople trooped back to turn in our ads and report on the worsening road conditions. At three o'clock, our ad manager suggested we all head home.

David left the mall where his store was. A few minutes after I pulled into the carport, his car slid into the stall beside mine.

A cup of hot chocolate later, we snuggled next to each other on the sofa. This, we were convinced, would be a beautiful Christmas.

"What a great time to be leaving!" he howled. "Florida, here we come!" On Sunday, we would board a flight to West Palm Beach, and Monday would find us celebrating Christmas with my family.

But the snow, scheduled to let up early Saturday, did not quit until late in the day. Night fell, along with the mercury, and while temperatures plummeted to sub-zero, the wind picked up at an alarming pace. The airport closed.

Entertaining Guests

Sunday we called every thirty minutes. The message never changed. By Sunday evening, we realized the finality of our situation: We were grounded.

Oh, I tried to be merry on Christmas. But I had never spent a Christmas without my mother and sisters. No matter how poor we were—like the year we were the charity family at our church—or how far apart—we managed to come together at Christmas.

After breakfast and opening gifts, David padded back to bed for a nap. I tried to read a new book, but my mind kept wandering.

In a pile by the front door were all the presents we had packed to take to Florida. On top of the stack was a one-pound box of Godiva chocolates. The shiny gold foil twinkled at me. It was for my family. I really shouldn't . . .

When David woke up an hour later, the box and I were sitting on the sofa together.

"Hey, how much of that did you eat?"

I tried to be casual. "Not a single piece."

He opened the lid. I was telling the truth. I hadn't eaten a single piece, but I had bitten off the top of every piece of chocolate in the box.

"Just checking! Just testing!" I mounted my defense. "This way everyone will know what they're getting!"

Entertaining Guests

Since then, we've stayed home more Christmases than we've traveled. Perhaps the snow that year was the cosmic jumpstart we needed to start our own traditions.

Being a Jewish and Christian family, we've been forced to create celebrations that are meaningful to both of us.

For Hanukkah, we light the candles, sing songs and spin dreidels. Each of the eight nights, Michael opens a gift—usually a book—with the last night being a "big" gift. Throughout December, we open the windows of the Advent calendar, and the night before Christmas, we watch our favorite Christmas movies, including A Tree Grows in Brooklyn and The Grinch Who Stole Christmas. On Christmas Day, we open our gifts and watch movies.

Each year, I write Michael a letter, telling him how much he has grown, what he has accomplished and how much we love him.

And, of course, every Christmas we buy a big box of Godiva chocolates. But David makes sure that I am never left alone in the same room with the box.

Entertaining Guests

BLESSING

*The spirit of Christmas is within me
and I can share it with everyone,
wherever I may be, using whatever tools
I have at hand.*

1) What holidays have a great family tradition in your life?

_____

_____

_____

2) What makes that tradition meaningful to you?

_____

_____

_____

*3) Have you ever been unable to celebrate that tradition? What did
you do to keep the spirit of the memory alive?*

_____

_____

_____

*4) How can you keep the spirit of the holidays while doing
something different?*

_____

_____

_____

Why Great Danes Don't Eat Dip

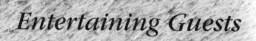

Tiffany and Bill loved their Great Dane Haliburt. But when mealtime came, Haliburt knew he wouldn't get table scraps. Haliburt had a delicate stomach. Still, when visitors showed up, Haliburt worked them over. Between longing gazes and soulful looks, the huge black beast made his wishes known.

One Sunday, Tif and Bill invited two couples to watch a football game on TV and then to eat a "tailgate" meal. Big bowls of chips and dip sat on every table in the TV room. Tif had prepared all the classic American dips: Dried onion soup with cream cheese, refried beans with guacamole and cheese, and artichoke hearts with sour cream in a hollowed-out loaf of bread.

During half-time, the crowd moved into the dining room to feast from six-foot-long submarine sandwiches, potato chips and beer.

"Somehow, I forgot all about Haliburt and the snacks in the TV room. He must have been tuned in because he was not only sneaky but also very quiet," said Tif.

After half-time, the crowd meandered back to the TV room only to find the dip bowls licked clean. A few crumbs were all that remained of the bread bowl.

Entertaining Guests

"We had a good laugh," Bill added, "And we settled down for the second half."

Unfortunately Haliburt's stomach was doing an end zone dance of its own.

First came the gas.

"Do you know how bad it can smell when a 200-pound Great Dane breaks wind?" asked Tif. "Suffice it to say, opening the patio door did not help."

Putting Haliburt outside would not work either. The temperature was well below zero and Danes have a thin coat of fur.

Bill grimaced, "So, we turned on the vent in the guest bath and lit five candles. Our friends laughed and we did too. I guess we laughed too soon...

"Because Haliburt then stood up, careened to the center of the room and began to heave!"

Tif and Bill both shoved the shaking Dane outside. Two inches out the door, Haliburt hurled.

"Our friends sat dumbfounded. That darn dog must have puked through two or three big plays, but nobody saw anything. We were transfixed by the sight of Haliburt," Bill remembered.

Entertaining Guests

Now, when Bill and Tif invite guests over to watch football on TV, Haliburt finds himself locked in the laundry room, while the story of the day the Great Dane ate all the goodies is told... with relish?

Entertaining Guests

BLESSING

What a gift humor is. I am grateful for situations in my life that can make me laugh.

1) What situations in your life have made you miserable?

_____

_____

_____

_____

_____

_____

_____

2) How could you have changed your attitude to open the way for humor?

_____

_____

_____

_____

_____

_____

_____

Entertaining Guests

3) *Think of a time when you laughed at something that could have made you mad or sad. How did the humor diffuse the situation and give it a positive twist?*

_____

_____

_____

_____

_____

_____

_____

Hoosier Hospitality

Camilla called us to her table and pointed out the dishes she'd cooked. There was fried eggplant, two kinds of rice, stuffed grape leaves, French fries with lentils, tomato and cucumber salad, and wheat patties. My mouth watered with anticipation. It had been 25 years since I had had a home-cooked Persian meal. I made myself go last in line so I wouldn't be a total pig.

As we ooohed and aaahed our way through the feast, the talk naturally turned to ingredients and cooking methods. Ramin, Camilla's husband, accepted our compliments on his wife's cooking and acknowledged that she had outdone herself. Then Jan's husband Bill noted that she was an accomplished Italian cook. As all eyes traveled to David, he looked at me and stuttered, "Joanna's a good cook, but I don't think she specializes in any particular nationality of food. Do you, hon?"

I laughed. "I'm trying to learn to cook all sorts of food, but if you are talking about cooking the food you grew up with, let's just say I can make a mean kidney bean salad."

Jan's jaw dropped. "Kidney beans? Those little pink things?"

"Yeah, they are a Hoosier dish." (Hoosiers are from Indiana.)

Entertaining Guests

Camilla's face froze. Obviously, she was trying not to express her true emotions. "Aren't they curved? Like half-moons? I didn't know you could make salad out of them."

Now, I had them. I had set the hook, so to speak, and the live ones were on my line. Time to reel in my catch. "Yes, but I think of them as more of a maroon color. Why don't you come over to my house and I'll make a bowl for you."

A date was selected, and our plans were made. Jan and Camilla arrived at the appointed time. If I do say so myself, Martha Stewart would have been proud. The kitchen table was covered with a lovely blue tablecloth embroidered with butterflies. In the center of the table was a small bouquet of flowers I'd picked from my garden. For our meal I'd made hot crab dip, cucumber sandwiches, curried tuna fish sandwiches, miniature quiches, fruit salad, and TA-DA: Kidney Bean Salad. Being the perfect ladies they were, both Jan and Camilla tried a little bit of everything.

After her second mouthful of kidney bean salad, Jan paused to examine her plate more carefully. "You know," she said, "this stuff *is* good. I would have never believed it, but it is."

Camilla nodded her head thoughtfully. "It is good. How do you make it?"

Entertaining Guests

I doubt that you'll run across this in any gourmet magazines, and I know you, too, may feel the need to impress your friends with your culinary expertise, so...

KIDNEY BEAN SALAD

1/4 cup finely chopped onion
3 T of sweet pickle relish
3 T of mayonnaise
1 hardboiled egg, chopped
1 can of kidney beans, rinsed

Mix well. Best if you let it sit overnight to absorb the flavors. Play with the relish and mayo to get the flavor you like best.

NOTE: Growing up, we didn't rinse the beans. We simply added the juice from the can. Since then, I've heard various theories on what that juice really is, so I rinse my beans in a colander now.

Entertaining Guests

BLESSING

Please help me not to discard or ignore what makes me who I am simply because I may not see what makes me special.

1) What recipe do you know by heart that you have never written down?

_____

_____

_____

_____

_____

_____

_____

2) What food or dish was a staple of your household?

_____

_____

_____

_____

_____

_____

_____

Entertaining Guests

3) What event or special activity from your past might seem embarrassing or silly to you today?

_____

_____

_____

_____

_____

_____

_____

4) Plan a party with friends. What might you cook that you ate a lot of when growing up?

_____

_____

_____

_____

_____

_____

_____

The Handyman's Special

M oving into a fixer-upper home gave Lyndsey and Pete their first desire to entertain.

"Until then, our poverty-stricken apartment in student housing was too embarrassing to want to share," said Pete. "But the first four weeks in our crackerbox house found us scrubbing, painting and decorating to beat the band. Lyndsey and I were so proud that we couldn't wait to show our parents how well we'd done."

Lyndsey leaned over and smiled conspiratorially, "See, they thought the house we chose was too much work. But all we could see was potential. They saw the headaches."

That Sunday morning, the two put the finishing touches on the re-wallpapered bathroom, hung up the towel rack, and put up the new shower curtain. Admiring their handiwork, they stopped for a doughnut and a quick peek at the Sunday paper. Inside, was an advertisement for an elegant brass-finished lighting fixture at a local hardware store.

"Wouldn't this look great over the dining room table?" asked Lyndsey. And before you could say, "Tool Time," the young couple had purchased the fixture and was starting to take down the old swinging bulb.

Entertaining Guests

"Do you think we should call an electrician?" asked Lyndsey, "Of course, we probably can't get this installed for a couple of weeks...."

Pete shook his head. "How hard can it be? I'll turn off the circuits and follow the directions. We'll save lots of money."

Unfortunately, mounting the new fixture was more difficult than it looked. The brass-finished, six-armed light was heavy.

"I'm pretty sure I got it anchored in a stud," Pete assured Lyndsey.

By then, Lyndsey was up to her elbows tossing salad to go with the spaghetti and meatballs. "I'm sure it will be fine, honey," she called out from the kitchen.

Pete's parents were impressed. The kids' work made a cozy cottage out of what the real estate agent had privately called "a dump." Pete ushered his folks into the dining room while Lyndsey carried in the spaghetti, covered with a steaming mound of sauce.

Proudly, she slid the bowl to the center of the table. They bowed their heads and gave thanks. As they chorused a hearty "Amen," they heard an equally loud SPLAT.

Entertaining Guests

By the lights of a passing car, they could make out the light fixture sitting in the middle of the spaghetti bowl. From the ceiling dangled ripped electrical wires.

"Uh, hum," chimed Pete's dad. "Get your coats, kids. Dinner's on me."

Lyndsey smiled as she remembered her father-in-law's kindness. "He was a gem. Later, he even paid to have an electrician come install the fixture for us."

"But," Pete added, "He didn't have to. I could have handled it. Really."

Entertaining Guests

BLESSING

There are people around me who can help.
Teach me to be willing to ask
for assistance.

1) Write down a situation in which you did not ask for help but really needed it. How was the experience? Did you really save on money or time in the end?

_____

_____

_____

_____

2) Write down experiences in which you have requested help. How did this make you feel? How did it make the person helping you feel?

_____

_____

_____

_____

3) List the positive results of asking for help. Pin them on your fridge.

_____

_____

_____

_____

Kid Stuff

All Children Need Comforting

Every April the homeowners on our block started to plant geraniums in front of their houses. This was my cue to go and buy geraniums, because every single neighbor was a better gardener than I. They knew when the danger of frost was past, and I knew to watch their cultivation closely. When the blooming geraniums lined my street, a trip to the garden center was in order.

My son Michael surprised me one year by offering to dig the holes for my plants. I pointed out the places where I wanted the holes and began to move the flats of geraniums from the trunk of the car. By the time I made it back to where Michael was digging, he'd created a good-sized hole, and dirt was piled neatly to one side along with the remains of my clematis.

That silly clematis had been planted four years earlier. I had babied it. I had tied it up. I had fertilized it. But each year, it steadfastly refused to bloom. So when I saw vestiges of the vine and a solitary blossom heaped with dirt beside the hole, I gnashed my teeth. Michael was surveying his handiwork with pride. I thanked him and cleared away the rubbish.

Later, I shared the whole incident with my friend, Elaine. "Can you believe," I moaned, "that after four years that clematis finally began to bloom, and Michael dug it up?"

Kid Stuff

Elaine's green eyes sparkled with mischief. "Heck, I think it deserved to be dug up. Four years is too long to wait. Michael did you a favor."

That's what good friends do for you. They make situations better, not worse. After all, the damage was done. Elaine could have suggested Michael needed pointers on digging holes. Or she could have said, "Why didn't you supervise him more carefully?" But instead, she chose a comment that made me laugh and put the upset in perspective.

By the way, that clematis was a pukey color of washed out lavender. Why on earth did I wait four years for that?

Kid Stuff

BLESSING

I am grateful for true friends. We can be a comfort to each other. Teach me the skills to make it better, not bitter.

1) What is your usual reaction to a problem? Imagine what you would have said about the dug up flower.

_____

_____

_____

_____

2) Who comforts you? How?

_____

_____

_____

_____

_____

3) Think of times you've been comforted. What skills were involved?

_____

_____

_____

_____

_____

Kid Stuff

4) When a friend is not available, how do you typically comfort yourself? Is that healthy?

_____
_____
_____
_____
_____
_____
_____

5) Write down phrases that you find comforting.

_____
_____
_____
_____
_____
_____
_____

Kid Stuff

Rocking Around the Clock

P arenting books are great. With few exceptions, you should read them once and then throw them away.

One book I read suggested that holding your child too much would create a dependent child. The expert noted that while a child is on your lap, he is not actively exploring and conquering the world around him. Parents who rock a child at night run the risk of making the child dependent on the rocking to get to sleep.

Shortly after reading this passage, we were invited to have dinner with another couple, the parents of a sixteen-year-old boy. When the young man introduced himself, I mentally compared his size with that of my then three-year-old son. Bart's hands engulfed mine when we were introduced. His feet recalled images of Bozo the Clown. I had to crane my neck back to look into his eyes as we spoke. His shirt was tucked in at the front of his pants and flapping out from his backside. Feeling shy before these strangers, Michael climbed into my lap, snuggled down and delighted me by how well he fit beneath my chin.

After dinner, I helped our hostess, Liz, clean up the dishes. In the congenial and familiar effort of clearing the table, we fell into "girl talk" with ease. As the surface emptied, Bart

Kid Stuff

spread his school books on the dining room table. Pleased by the warmth between mother and son, I told Liz about the book I'd been reading on parenting.

"Do you think it's wrong to rock a child too much?" I asked.

Liz smiled and beckoned me to the dining room. As Bart bent over his calculus homework, she embraced him from behind and planted a quick peck on the side of his cheek.

"Look at him. He's a great galoot. If I want to hold him or kiss him, I have to tackle him first. Rock him? I rocked him every chance I got and I'd do it again right now if I could," and her eyes grew shiny and wet.

"Ah, Mom."

Liz ruffled Bart's hair and cleared away an empty glass near her son's hand. "I say, rock them. Rock them every chance you get. They grow so fast."

Kid Stuff

BLESSING

Let me show my child how much I love him with every chance I get. Remind me that physical contact is healing and affirming in all relationships.

1) *Were you ever rocked? What do you remember about it?*

_____
_____
_____
_____

2) *When do you feel close to your child? What activity brings you close?*

_____
_____
_____
_____

3) *Plan something to show your child that you love him/her every day.*

_____
_____
_____
_____
_____
_____

Kid Stuff

Geez Louise!

My son mastered an ugly epithet. When he first uttered this expletive in my presence, I calmly explained the meaning of what he had said and why I found it offensive.

"That should be that," I thought to myself, feeling like a model parent.

Then he said it again. We went the disciplinary rounds: fines, punishments, time outs, and yelling. Yes, we yelled at him. This nasty little word so frustrated my husband and me that we would shout, "We told you NEVER to say that." So of course, he kept saying it. Oh, it would disappear for a few days, only to reappear in time to make us crazy. Or it would surface at the most unsettling times, like right after going to church. Try as we might, neither my husband nor I could eradicate this determined verbal weed.

Now, I know parents who believe their children should spend the bulk of their time at home. "We know our values, and we know what we want to teach them," says a friend of mine. "Outside the home, we have no control over what they learn. So we like them to spend all their free time with us as a family."

Kid Stuff

That would drive me nuts. I love having time to myself. I enjoy having time with my husband. I know my son needs time away from us.

When your child is with another family, you still have control. Inside your child's head, your voice plays the tapes of all you've said. Your rules are compared to other family's rules. Your child tries his or her social skills and learns what works. Then he returns home to discuss his discoveries with you. Of course, you don't want your kid to go just anywhere with just anyone, so when your child is young, you need to do a lot of picking and choosing whom he or she plays with. Those playmates, their parents, and their family help you teach your child. They help you drive home the points you make, or they give your child the chance to explore other options.

My son's best friends are two brothers, one in my son's grade and one a grade lower. The three boys hang out like the three musketeers. My initial concern was that in any group of three, someone always gets left out. Instead, in this group of three, two boys keep the third in line and they take turns in all those roles of mischief-maker, voice-of-reason, and back-up man. My son has blossomed this year, thanks to the friendship he's enjoyed with these brothers. When the opportunity came up for my Michael to go with them to their aunt and uncle's house, I was pleased. First of all, I was pleased for Michael to be

Kid Stuff

included because I love seeing him with his buddies. Then too, I was pleased because I like and admire this family.

On the other hand, I was less than pleased when Michael came home and reported that he had shared his "bad word" within hearing of the boys' aunt. In fact, I was so unhappy that I wanted to crawl under the porch and hide. Fortunately, my back was turned and Michael didn't see my face turn purple and then red as he reported that she had firmly asked, "Please don't say that in my house."

"Michael," I said, "Haven't we told you and told you not to say that?"

He mumbled, "Yeah."

You know what? He's never said that "dirty word" since.

I suppose that our kids don't realize why we fuss at them. I'm sure Michael thought David and I were being silly. Silly had nothing to do with it. We wanted to save him embarrassment, as well as mold his personal habits. As awful as I feel about someone else hearing my son's mistake, I am equally thrilled she reprimanded him. By being away from home and seeing that the rules of polite conduct are universal, Michael Slan learned a valuable lesson, one we had struggled to teach him.

Kid Stuff

BLESSING

*Thank you for other parents and friends
who support me in raising my child. Help
our children to see the love that is behind the
boundaries we set for them.*

*1) Write about a time that you were corrected by someone other
than family for doing something.*

_____

_____

_____

_____

*2) How did it feel to be in this situation? Did it make you angry
with your parents?*

_____

_____

_____

*3) Write down a challenge that you're working on at home with
your child. List some ideas for finding outside support for this
challenge.*

_____

_____

_____

_____

Kid Stuff

Glimpses of Who My Child Will Be

Although my husband looks like a single parent during the months when I'm traveling to book shows and scrapbooking conventions, come late November, our situation reverses.

David's business (selling Steinway pianos) goes gangbusters right before Christmas. After fourteen years of marriage, you would think I'd adjust to his absence during the holidays. I don't.

I find myself wishing that he could come with me to the mall to watch Michael talk to Santa. I grow misty-eyed as I watch husbands and wives Christmas shopping for their kids at Toys-R-Us while I comb the aisles alone. And, in the evenings that come so soon, I mope around arranging poinsettias, holly and presents.... solo.

Which still didn't excuse me for getting irritable with Michael once when his friend canceled out their Saturday play date.

"Mom, could you play War?" Halfway through, when his four aces, queens and kings were all in my possession, Michael threw a hissy fit and quit.

He cried for fifteen minutes.

Kid Stuff

"Mom, will you play Legos?"

I had my fill after we put together the 120-piece king's carriage. Michael started to whine that he was bored.

No, he did not want to go for a walk. No, he did not want to play computer games. No, no, no!

Then I lost it.

"I am not your personal play slave! Do you think I'm happy Frankie can't visit? Do you think I want to spend my Saturday playing Legos? Knock it off! Go play by yourself."

His retreating back stomped up the stairs just as the phone rang.

"This is Timmy. Can Michael come over and play?"

Faster than you can say Power Rangers, we were backing out of the garage and on the way to Timmy's house. As we pulled out of our subdivision, Michael said, "Mom? I guess I was really disappointed about Frankie. Sorry I made such a fuss."

As I squinted at him in the sunlight, I caught a glimpse of the person my son was becoming. We must be doing something right, I thought, for him to empathize with my feelings and take responsibility for his own,

For many months, I carried that moment in my head and turned it over and over like a lucky charm. A road sign

Kid Stuff

saying my destination was ten miles ahead could not have been any clearer.

That glimpse was a gift. I know David and I are on the right track, because I like the young man who is growing up in our house.

Kid Stuff

BLESSING

*I am living my life in the best way that I
know how. Thank you for the little moments
that show me that I am on the right path.*

*1) When have you had glimpses of maturity in yourself or in
family members?*

_____

_____

_____

_____

_____

2) Write down any incident that uplifted your spirits.

_____

_____

_____

_____

_____

My Whole Life

"**M**y whole life is in here," said Joon Ho solemnly as he handed me a wadded up piece of flip chart paper. "My whole life." He watched as I opened my purse and put the paper inside. He stood statue-like until I pulled the drawstrings and snapped the closure barricading his paper inside my portable Fort Knox.

I hesitated before speaking and my son Michael pushed past me on the way to the car. He sighed a teenage sigh, too worldly for an eleven-year-old, yet oddly right for the moment. "It's a time line we did in Sunday school. That's what he means." Before I can query him, Michael added, "It was dumb. I threw mine away."

Joon Ho's face never changed. He slumped into the back seat of the car and murmured, "My whole life. You can see my whole life."

How do you tell an eleven-year-old boy that he hasn't lived his whole life? Because he weighs more than I do and stands eyeball-to-eyeball with me, he must feel that he, too, is an adult. Yet, he isn't. At age eleven, there was so much more to come.

I struggled to honor the parental duality of the moment: to him, his life was sage, old and long; To me, he was a child

with a new crop of facial hair and acne, but little more than a baby, really. The problems which consternated him—whether to invite girls to his birthday party or how to get the rest of his science fair team to listen to his ideas—seemed trivial to me and earth-shaking to him. How could I give him the serious attention he requested, while reminding myself, "This too shall pass?"

How do you help a child bear the "slings and arrows" of childhood while remembering that this time is fleeting? The balancing act is tenuous. I struggle to give appropriate attention to the boys' hurts while reminding myself that tomorrow most of these will be forgotten. Childhood batters the heartiest of souls, but youth compensates with speedy and focused amnesia.

As his new "American Mom," I listened to Joon Ho's daily ups and downs, trying to temper my responses. The trick was not to make too big of a deal out of a situation he would soon conquer and forget. For example, when the students in his language class teased him for having difficulty translating from his native Korean to English and then to German, I was incensed. Part of me wanted to storm down to the school and knock all their little heads together. Joon Ho was juggling three languages. They were only coping with two.

Then I reminded myself that this was typical kid behavior. Nothing more, and little less. As I calmed myself, he went on to tell me with pride that he stood up for himself. He

Kid Stuff

said, "I told them to come to Korea, and we'd see how they did." A wave of pride overtook the anger. In a quick three months in our home, he had found his "sea legs." He didn't need my intervention.

Then I reconsidered the situation. "Joon Ho, they only tease you because they've forgotten that English isn't your native language. You are so much a part of the class that they expect you to keep up with them."

His face relaxed. Then his eyes lit up and he smiled.

Of all that I need to remember as a grown-up, I'd nearly forgotten the most important lesson of my own childhood. All children want to feel accepted. Whether from Korea or the United States, whether tall or short or smart or average, all children want to be a part of the group. Come to think of it, that's all most of us adults want, too.

Kid Stuff

BLESSING

Tough times will pass. Our troubles seem monumental to us, but I can remember that this too shall pass. In this way, I can also show compassion for the tribulations of others.

1) Do you remember a difficult time in your life that you thought would never pass? Write about it.

_____

_____

_____

_____

_____

2) How can you comfort your child while living through a tough time? Make a list.

_____

_____

_____

_____

3) How do you balance the short-term problems of your life with an eye to the long-term?

_____

_____

_____

_____

Unexpected Gifts

Unexpected Gifts

The Great Grape Adventure

While walking to the kitchen, I noticed the small portable vacuum cleaner sitting in the center of the living room carpet. Its cord stretched from the socket across the room. No boys were in sight. For a quick moment, I wondered what was going on. Then the timer went off in the kitchen and I hurried to turn over the chicken nuggets baking in the oven.

When I turned around, I noticed a box of Tide sitting on the kitchen island. In the sink was a crumpled rag. By the side of the sink was a tiny trickle of purple.

I called the boys up from the basement.

"What's going on?" I asked. They looked at each other. They looked at me. They looked at their feet. Then they mumbled, "Nothing."

"Why is the vacuum cleaner in the middle of the living room floor?" I persisted.

"We were just cleaning up," ventured Michael. Then, he broke. He began to jabber like a blue jay near a bird feeder. "And it was Joon Ho's fault and I told him not to and he told me not to tell and I think we got it all up."

Joon Ho was violently shaking his head at this point. "Not my fault! Not my fault!"

Unexpected Gifts

I never did figure out whose fault it was. I didn't care. The rule was no eating outside of the kitchen. The problem was purple grape juice spilled on my white living room carpet and white sofa. Of all foods, the boys decided on the one liquid most likely to leave a permanent stain.

Miraculously, the boys had managed to get up the majority of the color. Dissolving a small amount of Tide in water, they had made a cleaning liquid and attacked the dribble with a great deal of effort. Most of the purple had come out. But, there will always be a light violet shadow on the sofa and the carpet. Unless we re-carpet or recover our sofa, that stain is permanent.

After the boys were in bed that night, the school called. In three short months, Joon Ho would be returning to Korea. A snag in the visa process was to take him home to his parents six months earlier than we had all planned. Over the time of Joon Ho's stay, Michael had become dependent on his new "brother." In the months we'd spent together, Joon Ho had—on occasion—called me "Mom." We hadn't planned to say goodbye so quickly, and yet we would do so.

I sat down on the sofa to think. Outside the stars twinkled gently over our lawn. The dog sighed and lay down at my feet. The whole house had become quiet. Then the moon shifted from behind a cloud and filled the room with brightness. I looked down and saw the stain. In the dim light, it was barely visible, almost like it had never happened. Somehow, I was glad that faint reminder was there.

Unexpected Gifts

BLESSING

*Help me to focus on the important things
in life. Let us each leave our traces behind
so those we love never forget us.*

*1) Think of some mark you may leave behind. What might that
mark look like? What may others remember about you?*

_____

_____

_____

_____

*2) What traces have people left you? How do you remember others
who have moved out of your life?*

_____

_____

_____

_____

_____

_____

_____

Unexpected Gifts

Because I've Had You

On our way to Arlene Slan's room, we stopped by the nurses' station. As luck would have it, her doctor sat at the desk filling out her chart.

His face fell as he looked at David. "She's not doing well, not well at all. Frankly, she hasn't taken in enough food or water to stay alive. She's outlived all our best predictions."

Usually, the nurses gave Arlene morphine in the afternoon, but in a brief rally of consciousness, she had asked them to wait until after our visit. Arlene had wanted to be fully alert for us, even if that meant alert with great pain.

"I think you should know, David," explained the doctor, running his hand nervously through his hair, "This will probably be the last time you see your mother alive."

We walked together, hand in hand, down the long, sterile hallway with its stainless steel railing. David and I turned the corner and walked quietly into the room where Arlene Slan, or what was left of her, lay dying of cancer.

"I don't mind the dying," she had told me. "But the indignity just kills me," and she giggled. Arlene. So brave. Such a sense of humor. So gracious in death, that the membership of the temple joked that Arlene consoled even the rabbi.

Unexpected Gifts

Tubes ran from both sides of her. Her feet were bloated and splotchy. Her lips were cracked and her teeth were streaked with blood.

David let go of my hand and walked to her bedside. Gently, so as not to cause her pain, he lowered himself to sit beside her. Her eyes fluttered open and she looked at the face of the son she had waited seven long years to have.

Yes, she and her husband had tried for seven years to have a baby. So nervous was she that she had scheduled a meeting with an adoption agency for the day after she saw the obstetrician. "I couldn't bear it if he told me it was a false alarm," she had said, "I just couldn't bear it."

Her hand moved slightly as she reached to touch David. She looked at him with infinite love. Too weak to talk, she raised her hand and traced his chin with her fingers. Her face said it all: Because I've had you, my life has been worthwhile.

For her, motherhood was the crowning glory of her life.

Although our son was born almost seven years later, Michael was conceived that day in the hospital at Arlene's bedside.

Unexpected Gifts

BLESSING

What a glorious and precious gift it is to have a child. God teaches us through our children, and through our parents. We can nurture them and love them and then we have to let them go.

1) Write down how you felt about having children when you were younger.

_____

_____

_____

_____

2) Write about the feeling you had when you learned you were going to have a baby.

_____

_____

_____

_____

3) What moments have given you the greatest joy?

_____

_____

_____

_____

Unexpected Gifts

A Birthday Gift of Grace

"If you could have any gift for your birthday, what would it be?" said my sister Margaret as her cell phone crackled and snapped.

How do you answer a question like that? I could think of lots of requests: a painless face lift, a house on the beach, or a new BMW convertible...

I guess I paused too long, because she interrupted my thoughts. "We're on the way back from the ob-gyn's office and guess what? I'm having labor induced on your birthday."

My heart fluttered in my chest. My niece would be born on my birthday! After years of moaning and groaning about not receiving my fair share of attention since my birthday often coincided with Father's Day, this was a bonanza. I'd definitely hit the "mother lode" of all possible celebratory extravaganzas. As an extra perk, here would be one family birthday I could always remember, guaranteed.

Then being my gloomy little self, I started to panic. Margaret's previous labors had not been easy. In between her first and second daughter, she had miscarried. Sure, I wanted a baby for my birthday, but was this safe? Was it what she wanted? Had my selfish thoughts somehow influenced her? I had, after

Unexpected Gifts

all, made the comment that having a baby only one day from my birthday was unfair.

Margaret put my fears to rest. The hospital had three other induced births planned and hers would tax their facility. "We already paid for the birthing suite," Margaret explained, "so it makes sense to change our date."

The next day, as the music stopped in exercise class, and we walked over to grab our hand weights, I yelled, "Announcement! I have an announcement. My sister is having a baby, and I'd appreciate your prayers." The confused looks softened as the other eleven women and the instructor considered my request. "She's had a hard time in the past," I continued, "and maybe I'm asking this for my superstitious self, but I'd appreciate your thoughts."

After class several women came over to ask for details and promise their support. I raced from the class to catch a plane so I could accompany my husband to a meeting of piano dealers in Memphis, Tennessee. That night at dinner, I kept excusing myself to call for details about Margaret's progress. Finally, my husband explained my nervousness. To my surprise, several of the gentlemen there fondly recalled the birth of their children. At intervals, people would ask, "What's the news?"

We were on the rooftop of the Peabody Hotel watching a peach and orange sunset when little Rebecca Grace entered the world. As I shared the news, a cheer went up from the crowd.

Unexpected Gifts

It occurs to me that so often we try to handle life's stresses and problems without asking others for help. It seemed bold to ask an exercise group to pray for my sister. I felt awkward telling a group of business people that I was following the progress of my niece's arrival. Yet, the next week a few women asked about the new baby as we pumped up our biceps. And upon leaving Memphis, one gentleman shyly added, "Congratulations again on your new niece." Perhaps, just as it takes a village to raise a child, it also takes a community to ease our minds, to travel with us in times of concern. All I know for sure is that by sharing my worries, I felt better, and I can't help but think that little Grace has already earned her name.

Unexpected Gifts

BLESSING

I am grateful to be a part of the family of humankind. I am never truly alone. Teach me to forego pride and reach out for help, whether it is toward others or through prayer.

1) Have you ever shared a concern like the one in the story? Write about the situation.

_____
_____
_____
_____
_____
_____
_____

2) What would keep you from telling others about a concern?

_____
_____
_____
_____
_____
_____
_____
_____
_____

Unexpected Gifts

3) Consider the groups of people who are part of your life. How much do you know about their personal lives? Why?

_____

_____

_____

_____

_____

_____

_____

_____

4) How would you feel if someone asked you to pray for them or for a life situation?

_____

_____

_____

_____

_____

_____

_____

_____

Unexpected Gifts

Olivia's Potato Salad

"Before you serve that potato salad, you might want to sprinkle a little paprika on the top," said Olivia.

I laughed. Obviously she assumed I'd spoon the potato salad out of the plastic container and put it in a bowl before serving it to my guests. That's Olivia. She's a whiz at presentation.

Now Nancy's fine at presentation as far as I know, but her real talent is calling steps. I've never had a better step aerobic teacher. A big part of her appeal is her uncanny ability to yell out the next step at the exact split second my mind is wondering what to do next.

Elaine does step, too, but I've never heard her call it. Elaine is the perfect travel companion. She's always up for an adventure, reads maps like most of us read *People* magazine, and she finds the best local restaurants wherever we travel.

My girlfriends have enviable talents. And I'm no slouch myself. I can find four-leaf clovers. Yep, I can walk and look down to spot the one four-leaf clover in a patch. I can stop to scan a patch and pull out four-leaf clovers by the fistful.

In my neighborhood, I'm often seen bottoms up as I peruse a waving group of green leaves. I really should take a vial of

Unexpected Gifts

water with me, because by the end of the walk, the clovers are often wilted and sorry looking. As often as possible, I give the clover away. After all, we can all use a little more luck.

One morning a voice inside whispered, "Give it to her." So, I approached a woman walking toward me with an outstretched hand. "This is for you," I said. She looked at me with a puzzled grimace. Then she saw the clover.

"It's got four leaves," she said slowly. She looked up at me from her hand as if to say, did you know about this?

"Yes," I said. "It's got four leaves, and it's for you. Have a nice day."

Seasons came and went and I continued my quest to round up all the available four-leaf clovers. I was walking and thinking about an article I wanted to write when a woman crossed the street and approached me.

"You don't remember," she said, "but about a year ago you gave me a four-leaf clover. My daughter was getting her driver's license that day, and I was really worried about her. So I gave her the clover and helped her put it inside her wallet. You know, she's never had an accident. Thank you."

I laughed. We both laughed. On an elemental level we knew the clover hadn't saved her daughter's life or her car's fenders. But it had saved one mother a little dab of worry. And, hey, I'm all for helping other moms. Even if all I can do is share a stem of clover.

Unexpected Gifts

BLESSING

Our talents are given to us to share. Make us
willing to extend ourselves to other people.

1) What is your special talent?

_____

_____

_____

_____

2) Do you have any lucky charms? What are they and how do
they soothe you?

_____

_____

_____

_____

_____

_____

3) Has someone ever surprised you with an unanticipated kind-
ness? Tell them thanks.

_____

_____

_____

_____

_____

Unexpected Gifts

Your Essential Nature

T he Saturday before Christmas I was doing a forearm stand in yoga class when I was seized with a fit of the giggles that brought me tumbling down. My mirth erupted from an upside-down glance at my T-shirt, a cat in a Santa hat with a legend reading, "Buster listened patiently to what the mice wanted for Christmas... then he ate them."

Now what the heck does this have to do with life? As I re-centered myself and waited for the other students to come down (with more grace than I had shown), I started thinking about our essential nature. The point of the T-shirt is you can't change the essential nature of a cat, can you? A cat will want to eat small creatures. No matter that you plead, shout with disgust, or swat the rodent from its mouth, the cat must answer to its true nature. A cat is a cat.

By the same token, kids will be kids. As I drove my son and his friends home from school one Friday, they made so much noise that I couldn't hear the radio. They were kids being kids. The essential nature of a pre-pubescent boy is loud-y and rowdy. Being around the three boys reminded me that my son isn't more or less noisy, but he is representative of guys his age.

Unexpected Gifts

Each of us has a true nature that shows in all we do. I scrapbook in part because it is my nature to want life to be "just so." When I scrap, I recreate memories, situations and events. I stage direct them. I make choices. I edit. Best of all, I can remember the good and downplay the bad. Then I write my version of history, knowing that with the archival products I use this version will last.

Thinking about my pages, I realize they not only hold clues to my nature but also to how I perceive the people in my life. A page with my friend Elaine cradling a baby reflects that I see her nurturing side. A picture of my dog Kevin sprawled on a cushion reminds me of his unabashed love of comfort. My last photo of my grandmother sitting like a queen in her new lounge chair wearing her pink housecoat and pajamas shows the imperious side of her.

What I choose to photograph reflects the world I see, and that too, underscores my essential nature. Once we learn to look for a person's essential nature, we pay better attention to the talents and gifts of everyone we come in contact with. My friend Julie understands sports. It's part of her essential nature to be a keen observer of play on the field. When we go to baseball games with Julie and Dan, Julie's ability makes her an unerring photographer. I've learned that if I want to take better sports photos, I need to follow her lead. When she points her camera, I follow suit.

Unexpected Gifts

Understanding essential nature offers us opportunities of appreciation while it keeps us from banging our heads against the wall. As a friend once told me, "Never teach a pig to sing. You'll go hoarse, and the pig will get annoyed." If it's not in a pig's essential nature, you're in for a long hog haul!

Unexpected Gifts

BLESSING

*Thank you for the gifts of our essential
nature. Help me to be mindful of these gifts
so I can better appreciate my talents
and those of others in my life.*

1) What is YOUR essential nature?

_____

_____

_____

_____

_____

2) How does it show up in your life?

_____

_____

_____

_____

_____

3) Think of a person you have conflict with. How are your essential natures similar or different?

_____

_____

_____

_____

_____

Unexpected Gifts

4) *Take time to appreciate the essential nature of your spouse or your children. How might you define them?*

_____

_____

_____

_____

_____

5) *Copy the essential nature of a person you admire. What can you learn from that person?*

_____

_____

_____

_____

_____

_____

_____

Perfection Correction

Perfection Correction

Flower Power

When the "For Sale" sign went up in the yard across the street, Marilyn felt a wave of relief. For the three years since she and Bud had moved into the neighborhood, Marilyn had agonized over the perfectly tended yard, the clean cars, and the mowed lawn at 2205 Pleasant Street. Each time she walked out her front door, the tidiness of the pristine white house across the street seemed to mock her.

By contrast, Marilyn and Bud constantly tripped over Hot Wheels cars scattered over the sidewalk, bats and balls hidden in the too long grass, and skateboards at the foot of the concrete stairs.

"Boys," Marilyn muttered. Yet, a part of her was secretly pleased. She loved being a mother. Her sons were growing tall and handsome, and although getting a kiss proved more and more difficult each day, there was no doubt that they loved their mama. The sly, furtive kisses before a sleep-over at a friends, a quick hug before bed, and the quick swats on her bottom left her no doubt that her boys were filled with affection.

Still, as they grew older Marilyn kept thinking, "This is the year. This year I'll have flowers."

Perfection Correction

No, she didn't mind the drooping grass that begged to be cut more regularly. The toys, while a hazard, warmed her heart by clearly announcing, "Kids." And, dirty cars were dirty cars. Geez, vehicles seemed a necessary evil. Now if she had owned a Mustang convertible instead of a Taurus wagon, she might feel differently. But, a station wagon was a mom car, and mom cars got dirty as they chugged their way through days filled with ball practice, sloppy snacks, and muddy shoes.

What bothered her was the lack of flowers. She peeked out the front curtains and looked for the third time that day at the red geraniums which lined her neighbor's walk. Above them dangled hanging baskets of ivy. In the window boxes pansies, petunias and ferns flourished.

Yes, 2205 Pleasant Street was a riot of blooming beauty. Only in the winter did the blossoms fade. At the first blink of spring, sleepy and unsure, daffodils and tulips popped up and shouted, "Hello!" From that moment on, the masses of color caressed the neat white house like a lover's hand.

By contrast, Marilyn had been nicknamed the "Charles Manson" of the botanical set. Local garden supply houses had begged her to go away and never return. Mr. Gottschalk, a kind old gent who sold plants from the greenhouse next to his home, had actually screamed at her one day when she brought in a sick fuchsia. "De mites! De mites!" he had bellowed. "You infest all my plants," he'd moaned.

Perfection Correction

One spring, she had planted row after row of ruffled pink petunias beside her walkway. In a week, they began to curl over. She bought tomato stakes and tied old nylons around each one to hold up their frothy heads. They still toppled over and spent most of the summer with their heads in the dirt. When fall came and she finally dug them up, Marilyn pulled up a plastic marker and noticed the information about the plants. "Cascade," it read, "perfect for hanging baskets. This showy blossom falls gently over to give a cascading appeal." She groaned and threw the tomato stakes away.

"I've got to know her secret," Marilyn whispered. Glancing at the bathroom mirror, she gave herself a quick once-over. She was presentable, but just barely. She slammed the front door and marched across the street. She took a deep breath and rapped on the neighbor's door.

A salt-and-pepper head full of curls appeared. "Yes? Oh! You're our neighbor! The one with all the boys! Do come in," and a liver-spotted hand opened the screen.

Georgia Delaney stood a mere four feet tall. Her green eyes snapped with delight. "I've meant to meet you for years. Now that Frankie is gone, and I'm moving, it seems almost too late, doesn't it?"

The two women sat down and began to talk as though they'd been friends for years. The hours passed, and Marilyn noticed the time on her wrist watch with a start. "Georgia, the boys

Perfection Correction

will be starving if I don't get home," she said. "But before I go, there's something I simply have to ask you. What do you do to get your flowers to grow? I mean, they're so gorgeous. I envy them every year. Please, won't you tell me the secret?"

Georgia rocked back in her chair with a puzzled expression on her face. "You are kidding, aren't you?"

Marilyn pressed her advantage. "I've never been more serious in my life."

Georgia took a deep breath. Her lips twisted into a smile. "Dear child, not only will I give you my secret, but I'll also give you my flowers." She struggled from the chair and gestured for Marilyn to follow. They picked their way through the packed boxes and into a back bedroom. There, packed in neat cartons, sat row after row of flowers—silk flowers.

"Frankie was in the silk flower business, bless his heart," said Georgia. "Why don't you take a carton or two home?"

Perfection Correction

BLESSING

Help me to get the facts before I jump to conclusions. Teach me not to compare my situation to that of others, because I can never know enough to be fair to either of us.

1) Write down the names of people you admire.

_____

_____

_____

_____

_____

_____

2) Think of the ways that you admire one of these people. Write down a question you'd like to ask this person.

_____

_____

_____

_____

_____

Perfection Correction

3) Rather than make assumptions, be a good researcher. Ask questions. (It's nice to start with the compliment, "I don't know how you do it."). Write down the response.

---

4) Remember a time when you misjudged a person or a situation. How did you learn the truth? What did you learn from this?

Perfection Correction

Happy Trails are Filled with Poop

"**D**o you have time to talk? I read your stories in the Chicken Soup books, and I was wondering if you could give me advice."

I recognized this voice. This woman called me ten days ago when I was on the way to pick up my kids from school. I suggested then that she e-mail me. When no correspondence popped up in my AOL account, I figured she'd found an answer closer to home. Now she was back and she sounded slightly more urgent.

I qualified my help. I'm not a therapist, I told her. I write books. That's it. Yes, I have done my share of motivational speaking. That doesn't mean I can help. I really have nothing special to offer.

"But motivational speakers know how to get people started," she said. "I mean, I can't get motivated to do anything. What am I supposed to say to myself? I just need to know what to do to straighten myself out. I had this baby, a year ago, and I can't get going."

First, I wondered, had she had a recent medical check up? Could she possibly be depressed?

Perfection Correction

"Depressed? But I have a baby and I'm married," she protested. "I'm just kind of having a hard time. That's all."

Exit fantasy. Enter real life. On the road to happy trails, you stepped in a steaming pile of horse poop. 'Cause no one told you that babies, even healthy ones, do not guarantee a happy ever after life. Marriages, even good ones, do not promise happy ever after, either. Having no "problems" isn't the same as having it made.

Children—even absolutely adorable babies—demand a lot of effort. Statistics show that marital satisfaction takes a dive after a baby is born. As Brad E. Sachs put it in his book *Things Just Haven't Been the Same: Making the Transition from Marriage to Parenthood,* "No matter how much we want them, and how hard we worked to get them, children create an enormous strain in our lives as individuals and couples. The conversion from husband and wife to father and mother is one that, particularly at first, has more negative than positive changes associated with it." Of course, we wouldn't want to admit that socially, would we? Instead, we rush up to new parents to tell them, "You're so lucky!"

And as a new parent, you know you are lucky, incredibly so. Yet you feel anxious, and so weighed down. You really, really wanted this baby. You prayed for it. It's healthy. How could you complain? How could you feel resentful? If you do, there must be something wrong with YOU. So, now you are caught

Perfection Correction

in a guilt sundae, one giant scoop of ingratitude topped with a generous dollop of guilt, smothered in the fear that God is going to get you. (I'll give you something to cry about!)

This young lady decided to beat up on herself. She thought her malaise showed weakness, not humanity. She thought that all she needed was to get motivated.

"You don't get any extra points in life for being miserable," I said. "Yes, you can tough it out, but why? If getting help might make you happier, won't you be a better wife and mother?"

That turned the tide.

She wouldn't get help for herself, to make her life easier, but gosh, her husband and baby did deserve more. We ended the conversation with her promise to talk to a doctor. I set down the phone and shook my head. Why are we women so willing to help everyone but ourselves? As Sachs says, "(Women) feel guilty about reaching for something that is for them rather than for others."

Perfection Correction

BLESSING

I can give myself permission to care for myself. I, too, am worthy of love and attention. I, too, have needs. Let me see that caring for myself is a sign of maturity, not selfishness.

1) What one thing, however simple, can you do every day to take care of yourself?

_____

_____

_____

_____

2) Computers have reboot disks — what can you create for your own personal reboot?

_____

_____

_____

_____

3) Write down a reboot operation that works for you and keep it where you can find it when you need it.

_____

_____

_____

_____

Perfection Correction

Find Ways To Win

I stepped over the toys as I made my way to the dresser in Michael's room. My son barely noticed my legs swinging one at a time over his head.

"Varooom!" he shouted. "And there he goes." Watching the tiny Hot Wheels car slide off the ramp, Michael gurgled with glee. "And Michael Slan wins for the best car hopping off the ramp."

Silently I put his shirts into the designated drawer, trying not to unfold them as I slipped them in. Shirts only stayed unwrinkled as they waited in neat piles. Once they were over my son's head and pulled down to his waist, a landscape of crevices appeared. Scootching on the floor, wiggling against sofa cushions, wiping off a messy face tended to wad up a freshly laundered shirt faster than you could say, "Change clothes." Being one of three girls, the unending physical energy of boys had once again caught me off-guard.

"Errrrrrk. Varroom. Varroooom," sang out Michael. The little car flipped over on its side halfway down the racetrack and came to a skidded halt on its side. "Oh, and Michael Slan wins for the best car driving on its side," Michael announced solemnly. Then he put down the tiny car and gave himself a rousing round of applause.

Perfection Correction

Behind him, I matched up socks and straightened the pile of underwear. The dividers in the drawers kept clothing items in discrete sections, but still they managed to migrate and mix on a daily basis. I flipped the underwear so that half had waistbands at the back of the drawer and half had waistbands at the front. This made the pants lie flatter. I separated the socks into colored dressy socks and plain white for everyday.

"Wow! Wow!" shouted Michael, "Look at that." As I looked over my shoulder, I saw his little car flip over twice and bounce along the track before landing upside down. "Michael Slan wins again for the best fancy driving. Unbelievable!"

I took a long breath and turned to correct my son. Cars win races because they speed down tracks on their wheels. Cars do not win because they flip off the tracks. This is not right. He's wrong. That's all there is to it. There's a right way and a wrong way. Period.

I hesitated. Maybe he was right, and I was wrong. I sat down on the edge of the bed and watched him play. My definition of right and wrong was very, very narrow. Clothes had to be in the drawer just right. Socks had to be separated. Cars—even play cars—had to drive along the straight and narrow to win. With the force of a punch to my stomach, I saw how hard I make it for me to succeed. On the other hand, Michael Slan had figured out lots of ways to win. Instead of correcting him, I could learn from him.

Perfection Correction

Life constantly offers me the chance to make a judgement. I pride myself on being a person with high standards. Maybe though, I've lifted the bar too high. Maybe I make impossible demands on myself and others. Maybe I sacrifice appreciation for what I have on the altar of what I don't have. Instead of looking for ways to correct actions by myself and others, perhaps I'd be better served if I, like Mike, looked for ways to win.

Strategic Coach Dan Sullivan calls this concept "the gap." Sullivan points out that most of us have an ideal, and as we journey along we compare our progress (Point B) not to where we started (Point A) but to that ideal far in the future. Of course, we fall short. No matter how far we've traveled from Point A, our ideal still lies before us. Like the horizon, the ideal moves out of reach, always and forever. Sullivan notes there are two kinds of people: Those who live in the moment and appreciate how far Point B is from Point A, and those who live in the future by comparing all current points to the distant horizon of the ideal.

Imagine this: My son at age eight teaching me about the joy of the journey. By watching him,, I was given the chance to see how to create a life of appreciation for my progress rather than despondency about my shortcomings.

Perfection Correction

BLESSING

Perfection is something we create in our minds. Help me to see the natural perfection around me.

1) List a current situation that has you feeling like you're losing.

_____
_____
_____
_____

2) List the ways that you have grown in this situation.

_____
_____
_____
_____
_____
_____

3) Are there ways in this situation that you are winning?

_____
_____
_____
_____

Thanksgiving at Cracker Barrel

As we tossed the turkey breast into the shopping cart, a wave of nostalgia swept over me. Or maybe it was heartburn from eating the sample of tofu guacamole passed out by the silver-haired lady in the produce aisle.

Growing up, Thanksgiving had always meant a big turkey. Mama made her onion and celery bread dressing. Grandma Marge made turkey giblet gravy. Together they would mix green beans, cream of mushroom soup and Durkee onions for a casserole. A pot of potatoes would boil on the range until they passed Mom's prick test, and then she would mash them vigorously with a tool my great-grandmother had used.

Thirty years later, I was cruising the shelves of the grocery store, looking for low-fat turkey gravy in a jar, low sodium green beans, and instant mashed potatoes.

Worse yet, David, Michael and I would eat alone. The rest of the family had relocated to Florida.

Hey, I told myself, concentrate on the good. You have each other. How you cook for this holiday is your choice, and it fits your lifestyle. Don't do this to yourself.

Had Charles Dickens lived longer, perhaps he would have written about the ghost of Thanksgiving past. After all, Thanksgiving

Perfection Correction

is such a uniquely American holiday that it serves as a barometer in most families. Lots of folks around the table = Happy family; Sparse crowd = Lonely people.

The next day dawned bright and glorious as any Thanksgiving I can ever remember. I rolled out of bed and strolled outside for my daily walk, thinking, "Wow, what a beautiful day! Here's something else to give thanks for."

David and I slid the turkey breast into the oven. Michael and I finished grinding carrots for the carrot cake David's mother used to make. I made a quick rendition of Mom's celery and onion bread dressing. The house filled with lovely fragrances like aromatic blessings.

Right before the buzzer signaled the bird was done, the phone rang. The Floridian branch checked in.

"What time are you all eating?" I asked. "Whose house will you be going to?"

My sister Margaret cleared her throat, "We're eating at Cracker Barrel."

"CRACKER BARREL?"

"Yes. Mom says she's tired of cooking Thanksgiving dinners after all these years. Jane is working late, so she can't help. The last two years Michael and I cooked and were exhausted by dinner time," she sighed. "So, this year it's Cracker Barrel."

Perfection Correction

We chatted for awhile and then the buzzer went off.

David, Michael and I gave thanks for our terrific, healthy meal and for each other.

The greatest blessing was the phone call from Florida. I guess home and family never change in your mind. I had almost cheated myself of the opportunity to enjoy what I had by longing for the past.

This year, I was thankful for "now". It is said there is a reason we call it the "present": It is God's gift to us.

Perfection Correction

BLESSING

Sometimes the greatest blessing is sitting right in front of me, right here and right now. Thank you for the wonderful people in my life and for all that I have.

1) *Think of a time that you worried about what might be or might have been. What happened?*

_____

_____

_____

_____

_____

2) *Count the blessings that you have right here and right now. Post them on your mirror or fridge or by your bed. Make a new habit of counting your blessings and expressing your gratitude for what you have in the present.*

_____

_____

_____

_____

_____

Perfection Correction

You Don't Have to Carve the Pumpkin

"Mrs. Slan. This is Theresa from Michael's school. Michael is fine now," she said, "Except that while he was playing outside today, he ran a stick into his eye."

"Fine?" I tried to keep from screaming.

"Oh, yes. His eye watered quite a bit, but now he's back outside playing."

My priorities did a big shift. Everything on my to-do list suddenly looked unimportant as I shuffled through the phone book for the phone number of the eye clinic.

I picked up Michael, took him to the doctor, heard that he was really, truly fine, and headed home. Then I remembered the pumpkin.

"Mom, I can still go trick-or-treating, can't I? It won't be too late, will it?" He looked at me in mounting horror as he contemplated a year gone by without a trash bag full of candy.

"Sure you can. We just need to put in your eye drops and get you some dinner and carve the pumpkin."

"Why?"

"Well, we bought that big pumpkin to make a jack o'lantern. If we don't carve it tonight, it will go to waste," I said, working

Perfection Correction

myself into a lather. Inside, a little voice kept hollering, "Gotta carve the pumpkin. Gotta get it done. Gotta make dinner. Gotta put in eye drops. Gotta...gotta...gotta..."

Michael looked at me and shook his head. "We don't gotta carve that pumpkin, Mom."

He was right. Sometimes I act like the good parent police are going to swoop down on my house and arrest me if I don't follow all the old routines: Sew a Halloween outfit from scratch, carve the pumpkin, roast the seeds, go trick-or-treating, and give out the best candy on the block.

The truth is I DON'T GOTTA DO NOTHING!

Pared down to its essence, all my son cared about was going trick-or-treating. Now, before his bewildered eyes, I was becoming a witch and I wasn't even wearing a costume. All for a lousy $15 pumpkin!

Seems to me like sometimes I treat life as a big to-do list. That's when I need to remember my friend Maggie Bedrosian and her advise, "Life is more than your to-do list." Or put another way, don't confuse your to-do list with your higher priorities.

Back at the house, we grabbed a couple of sandwiches. Michael put on his Halloween costume of Chinaman's hat, a Chinese silk jacket and blue jeans. When one bewildered man handed out candy and then asked what he was, Michael said, "I'm a trick-or-treater." Then he tossed his candy in his bag and smiled, "Happy Halloween!"

Perfection Correction

BLESSING

*Love is simple, so help me keep from
making live too complex. Guide me to get
rid of those notions that keep me from seeing the happiness waiting all around me.*

1) How do you make your life complex?

_____

_____

_____

_____

_____

_____

_____

2) What could you do to simplify and still have the quality of life
and relationships you desire?

_____

_____

_____

_____

_____

_____

_____

Perfection Correction

Of Centerfolds and Casseroles

My speaker friend Joe O'Rourke tells a story about his mom finding a copy of *Playboy* magazine in his room. "I explained to her that I looked at *Playboy* for the same reasons I looked at *National Geographic*—I wanted to see the places I would never get to visit!"

The female version of *Playboy* isn't *Playgirl*, surprise, surprise. It's *Bon Appetit.* Or, the food pages of *Family Circle, Redbook* or *Good Housekeeping*.

When my friends and I fantasize, our hormones hum at the sight of food, food we will never make and most certainly, will never eat.

You know you are in trouble when the recipe has more than six ingredients and a little editor's note on where to find half of them. Any concoction that causes the modern shopper to deviate from eye-level shelves in the market can be seen as an invitation to culinary chaos.

In contrast, the few books I own on balancing home and family suggest the working woman will save time and money by spending her weekends cooking casseroles. This news bewilders me. Casseroles?

Perfection Correction

When was I supposed to find the free time to cook casseroles during the weekend? Between laundry loads, piano lessons, gassing up the car, going to the supermarket and driving my son to play dates? Gee, maybe I should be getting up early to whip up a few pans of lasagna and tuna casserole instead of sleeping.

Furthermore, my family won't eat food that is mixed together. They don't trust me. If David and Michael can't identify each ingredient, the forks go down and silence reigns. Good food arrives on plates with little separate compartments like the old aluminum TV dinner pans. No mixing and matching allowed.

In my house, sauces are suspect. Serve any color but the tomato red of spaghetti sauce and the meal is over. They've learned that sauce covers a multitude of culinary sins, including pureed vegetables that *Parents'* magazine swears will go unnoticed.

But I reasoned, I must be the Lone on the Range-r. After all, every woman's magazine I buy devotes itself to page after page of mealtime masterpieces. So, I polled my working mom friends to ask, "What do you serve at your house? Are casseroles a mainstay?"

Sharon: "On weekends, once in a great while, I will make a double batch of lasagna and freeze half. That's it."

Melanie: "Barbeque. We keep the Weber on the deck. Dave will cook on it even when he is standing in snow. Gives me a break and the food tastes great."

Perfection Correction

All others: "Pizza." "McDonald's." "Sandwiches on the run." "Soup Starter in the crock pot."

Which leads me back to my original question: Who's making all those luscious delights? Single women? Mothers of budding gourmets? Moms with kids who have left the nest?

Here's my theory: Recipes are to women what centerfolds are to men. We look, we lick our lips, and we imagine ourselves enjoying.

:

Perfection Correction

BLESSING

*Life is full of fantasies. Fantasies remind
me of the importance of staying playful and
creative in my life. Grant me a sense of lightness as I go about living.*

1) Think of things you have to do on a daily basis.

_____
_____
_____
_____
_____
_____
_____

*2) Write down some creative ways to tackle them so you can
recapture playfulness in your life. Have fun with the choices.*

_____
_____
_____
_____
_____
_____
_____

Real Worlds

Real Worlds

Moving Forward with Faith

A preliminary exam by a recommended orthodontist turned up a concern more surprising than the need for braces: A tongue-tied child. Despite examinations by pediatricians and dentists, until this moment no one had noticed the thin film of skin that held Michael's tongue tightly to the bottom of his mouth.

"It's a five-minute clip job, and he'll be back at school the next day," said the orthodontist.

Two weeks later, we had an appointment with an oral surgeon. The morning was not auspicious. I had gone downstairs to let out the dog and arrived just in time to watch our guinea pig throw himself onto his side, take two quick kicks in the air and die.

"We've got to have a funeral for him," Michael insisted as tears rolled down his cheeks. I demurred. Some stubborn streak in me was positive that confounded rodent would, like Lazarus, rise again. Off and on during my day, I stopped by the cage to check, and still the critter didn't move. Drat.

Then, while making lunch, I sliced deeply into my thumb, creating a flap of skin that spurted blood. No matter what I did, the cut refused to stop bleeding. I drove to pick Michael

Real Worlds

up after school with one hand held above my head like an impatient student hoping to be called on.

The five-minute clip job was a bald-faced lie. First, there was the prepping and anesthetizing. Then the doctor cut loose my son's tongue. The "clip" required eight stitches. All in all, much more than we had bargained for. An hour and a half later, a dopey boy staggered to my car. Fifteen minutes later, he was moaning with pain. "I han't wallow," he whined when faced with a Tylenol with codeine. School the next day? Not hardly.

My son crawled into our bed for a restless night. After hours of complaining, Michael fell asleep at 11:30 p.m. I slipped away to the guest bedroom. At 1:30 a.m., he awakened in pain. By 2:30 a.m., he was back asleep. At 4:30 a.m. the dog puked on David's side of the bed. At 5:30 a.m. David gave up trying to sleep and dressed for work. Dizzy with lack of sleep, David drove past the video store on his way to work, forgetting to return three late videos he'd had in his car for two days. On the way home, David forgot his promise to pick up dog food.

The morning of Day Two, Michael roused himself from bed and stood two inches from my face to announce, "I can't take this anymore." He hadn't brushed his teeth in two days. I managed to get his medicine down him. Every ten minutes, I answered a new request for water or ice cream or comfort.

Real Worlds

On one trip to let the dog out, I noticed a smell wafting from the cage of the dead guinea pig. Scheduling a proper burial was out of the question. I left Michael alone for half an hour to drive to the only nearby place we didn't owe late videos and picked up an entirely inappropriate movie for him. While Michael watched the PG-13 video, I triple-bagged the guinea pig and sneaked the offending carcass into the trash. As the lid slammed down on the green container, I bumped my thumb and re-opened the cut. As I pressed a rag to it, a raspy voice in another room called, "'Om? 'Om? 'Ould you make me 'icken soup?" The dog now took an aggressive stand between me and the pantry and whined, as if to say, "How about THE DOG, lady? I need to eat, too."

For a moment, I was overcome. I sank back against a counter-top as a sense of weakness flooded over me. "I can't take this any more," I heard myself say.

But another voice laughed, "Of course, you can. This is only temporary." Suddenly, I thought of Highway 40. If you live in St. Louis County and you travel east on I-40 to downtown St. Louis, you'll come over a hill at Mason Road where the morning sun fills your windshield and blinds you. For a few moments, you can't see a thing. The sun, like a myriad of problems, is all there is in the world. No cars to your left or right, no road before you. Nothing exists but the sun. For this fleeting moment, you must keep on keeping on. You must continue at a

Real Worlds

steady speed, not make any rash moves, and move forward with confidence, which comes from the Latin words "con" meaning "with" and "fidem" meaning "faith." You must move forward with confidence, even if you don't feel it, because you know this blindness is only temporary. Faith tells you that if you hang on, everything will be alright.

So I opened the pantry and pulled out the chicken soup. Yes, my son's mouth will heal, my thumb will quit dribbling blood, and the dog can feast on an old dried bagel. They don't come lock you up for late video rentals, and the guys at the city dump are skilled at burying dead pets. The small problems that seem so big right now are really not much more than the bright sun in my eyes at Mason Road. All I need is to go on with confidence.

Real Worlds

BLESSING

I can go forward with confidence.
Tribulations that temporarily blind me will
pass. I need to keep moving forward
steadily with faith.

*1) Think of a time when you were overwhelmed. What eventually
happened?*

_____

_____

_____

_____

*2) Consider a current challenging situation. Write affirmations of
faith to help you hang on.*

_____

_____

_____

_____

*3) If you are in an overwhelming situation, consider downmoding.
"Downmoding" is a term NASA uses to describe cutting back on the
planned activities. How could you downmode now?*

_____

_____

_____

_____

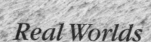

Real Worlds

The Case for Hiring Help

The heavy snowfall had kept the attendance light for my evening presentation of balancing family, career and self. Because there were only twenty-five women in the room, I suggested we begin by introducing ourselves and drawing a picture of what our lives were like.

Woman after woman spoke of needing perspective, of wanting better balance, and time for themselves and their families. The pictures showed happy houses, smiling faces and families holding hands. The last woman sat in the farthest corner of the room, her voice quiet as we strained to hear.

"I'm Lydia. I am a doctor. Here is a picture of the hospital where I work. I am the tiny face in this window. Outside in the sun are my husband and my daughter playing while I work. All I do is work, work, work. And when I get home, I do laundry and clean bathrooms." On that note, Lydia collapsed in tears.

Girlfriend, I am here to tell you that if you are working full-time, you deserve a cleaning person. Okay, you can't afford it. Do it anyway. Have a person come in once a month. Brown bag it to lunch every day. Make them eat meatless spaghetti or macaroni and cheese. Whatever it takes, get the help.

The money is not really stopping you. The real problem is that deep in our souls, we believe cleaning the house is our job. Say

Real Worlds

it loud and don't be proud: Cleaning houses is what being a woman is all about! Now, doesn't that sound silly?

Your mom did it all. Okay. But she didn't work 52 hours a week either. Plus, your dad probably waltzed into the house at exactly the same time every work day of his life.

Your husband wouldn't do it.

Martha told one of my groups about a pact she and Paul made. She and Paul would alternate cleaning the house on Saturdays. The first Saturday, she cleaned from 8 a.m. to 4:30 p.m. The second Saturday, she went to the mall and enjoyed herself although she wished Paul was with her. She returned to an impeccably clean house. That surprised her. The third Saturday, she cleaned all day and felt exhausted and irritable at the day's end. The fourth Saturday, she got half way to town when she realized she had forgotten her wallet, so she turned around and drove home. Martha walked into her kitchen and discovered A STRANGE WOMAN ON HER HANDS AND KNEES SCRUBBING. Paul was nowhere to be seen.

"Ooooohhh," gasped the other women in the session, "Weren't you mad at Paul?"

Martha hesitated, "Yes. A little. Then I got to thinking. I realized that he valued his free time more than I did. He knew I'd never consent to hiring help. But he wasn't going to give up his weekends because I felt guilty about getting help. He actually

Real Worlds

had done me a favor. Now the cleaning lady person comes every Saturday and Harry and I are having a ball!"

After another presentation on balance, a gentleman in his sixties waited to talk with me. "My mother did it all, so I thought my wife would be able to handle the workload also," he shared. "But, I forgot that Mom didn't work away from home an additional forty hours a week. Maybe I did not want to be honest with myself."

"Anyway, my wife took sick. Really sick. When she started to recover, one of the kids got the idea to pay for a cleaning service for her."

And after the woman had recovered, they kept the cleaning service anyway. To this gentleman's joy, the additional help considerably changed his wife's outlook on life.

"I got back the girl I married. I guess with the kids, the farm and her job, she wore down a bit at a time. I was an old fool not to notice, but by golly, I do now."

He leaned in and whispered to me, "Tell 'em, Joanna. You tell these young ones not to fuss about hiring help around the house. I almost waited too long. Don't let it happen to them."

Consider yourself told.

Real Worlds

BLESSING

*I have much abundance in my life. There
is enough money to obtain what
I need to make my life worthwhile.*

*1) Make a list of things you <u>need</u> (that would really make your
life better quality) in order to function happily and efficiently.
What would they cost?*

_____

_____

_____

_____

_____

_____

_____

*2) Now make a list of things you sometimes frivolously spend
money on (and the cost) that you could do without once in
a while. Total up the amount. Could that amount go toward
household help?*

_____

_____

_____

_____

_____

Real Worlds

Lose Those 10 Pounds

D on't ask me to find them, but I know I've filed at least a couple of surveys on women and weight. Most of us look at the scale and groan. We women often say to each other, "If I could only lose ten pounds…"

Which reminds me of a story I once heard about a woman who was saving a new outfit for when she lost ten pounds. One morning she stepped on the scales, and hey! She'd lost that dreaded extra-baggage. So, she slipped on her new outfit and waltzed off to work. All day long, people complimented her on how she looked. She confided gleefully about her weight loss. She beamed and looked terrific.

That night before she went to bed, she stepped back on the scale and discovered she had regained the ten pounds. Or had she? A little sleuthing and a few questions followed, and then she learned that her husband had re-adjusted the scale to show ten pounds lighter. Her morning reading had been incorrect.

The moral of the story? Is ten pounds all that stands between us and true happiness? Then we need to dump the ten pounds or get over it. Maybe those ten pounds are really a figment of our imagination.

Real Worlds

BLESSING

*My world is as I see it. I can shift my
perspective or I can change the situation.
It is up to me.*

1) What's bugging you?

_____
_____
_____
_____

2) What have you tried that has worked?

_____
_____
_____
_____

3) What have you tried that hasn't worked?

_____
_____
_____
_____

4) Gather all the information you can about your alternatives.
Pick an alternative and take the first step.

_____
_____

Real Worlds

Throw Out a Lifeline

The latest accessory for lifeguards isn't sunglasses, a sports watch or a cool tattoo. It's a 4-foot long rescue tube that guards sling over one shoulder and under the other arm. Upon spotting a flailing swimmer, the guard can dive into the water with the foam lifesaver trailing behind. This improvement on the O-shaped life rings tags along with less resistance than a circular shaped object. While at first, these funky logs seemed awkward to my eye, now I'm comforted by the sight of them.

Even the best swimmers can go under. I consider most of the mothers I know to be "good swimmers" as we navigate our way through life. We deal with impromptu schedule changes. We toss together meals at the spur of the moment. We assess situations with our kids and make snap decisions about how to discipline, encourage or ignore.

But all of us could use a lifeline once in a while. You can't always tell when another mother is bobbing under for the third time.

A few days before my labor with Michael, I had worked myself into a tizzy. I was scared of the potential pain. As with every first time mother, I was daunted by the upcoming experience. At nine months, you hum the theme song to "No Way Out"

Real Worlds

with every breath you take. My husband seemed unconcerned. My mother was on vacation with a friend. I had quietly worked myself into a panic when the phone rang. An acquaintance from our local temple called about an inconsequential matter. We concluded our business and then she asked, in an off-hand way, "How are you doing?" Inadvertently, she opened the floodgates. I poured out my fears to her. She listened calmly and without judgment.

When I had finished, she spoke in a low and reassuring voice. "Of course, you are scared," she said. "We're all scared going into motherhood. Especially facing labor. But Joanna," she paused as if gathering her thoughts, "look around you at all the people in the world. Remember that each of them is the product of a woman going through labor. It's frightening, but it's doable. You'll be fine."

I put the phone down gently. She was right. I would be fine. Although she wasn't a relative or a good friend, this woman had thrown me a lifeline. It meant all the difference in the world to me.

Real Worlds

BLESSING

Keep us ready, willing and able to toss out lifelines. Help us to listen to the fears of others. Grant us the wisdom to respond.

1) Think of a lifeline someone threw to you. Write about it.

_____

_____

_____

2) To be a useful lifeline, the comment must be non-judgmental. Brainstorm a few ways to broadcast a non-judgmental life line. For example, "I felt that way myself until I learned..."

_____

_____

_____

3) Write an affirmation for giving lifelines. It might go like this: "I am blessed with the opportunity to reach out to others."

_____

_____

_____

4) Think of a person who might need a lifeline right now. How can you reach out?

_____

_____

Real Worlds

Nell's Garden

I am a creature of habit. The walking route I've established never varies. As the days and weeks go by, the progressive changes of the landscape entrance me. On my walks, I take joy in what my fellow gardeners have planted. A hydrangea here, a frothy mound of Russian sage there, and a clump of coral geraniums along the way—well, I know the neighbors weren't thinking of me when they planted, but I still see their efforts as a gift. Of all the sights, I think I cherish Nell's Garden the most.

Nell's house sits on a corner lot. Like so many lots in our neighborhood, her backyard slopes steeply off from the foundation of her house. Since her corner lot is oddly-shaped, Nell has concentrated on her front yard. On either side of her curving driveway, she has planted and tended long beds of flowers. Every morning when I walk, I pass Nell on her knees paying homage to Mother Nature. So absorbed is she, that Nell rarely looks up. Her hands fly over the plants with a sureness that comes from knowledge. She discards weeds, dead-heads spent blossoms and prunes branches. While the other women on the block chat over coffee, Nell communes with her flowers in silence.

One morning Nell wasn't bent over the day lilies. She didn't attack her huge rose bushes with pruning shears. Nor did she tie

Real Worlds

back her clematis so it wouldn't droop over the front window. On this morning, Nell sat on her front porch looking lost. An empty coffee cup dangled from her left hand and dribbled a brown stream onto the concrete. Nell stared off into space. At first I thought she was comatose. After a long pause, her eyes merely blinked. Everything about her was still and frozen.

"Nell? Nell? Are you all right?"

Slowly she turned to stare at me without recognition. Then she looked back over the dry beds. With a long deep breath, she came to life and dropped her gaze to her feet. "Yes," she said in a whisper. "I'm fine. "

I waited. Some part of me sensed she was mustering the energy to share. I concentrated on standing motionless lest I startle her into running away like a doe on the edge of the forest. She looked as helpless and unsure as any wild animal I've ever seen. Then she opened her mouth, and after a long wait, she said, "We're moving."

Now I joined her in her despondency. I had come to view her garden as one of my personal highlights. What would I do without the fragrance and the flower heads nodding in time to my footfalls?

Three weeks later the real estate sign competed with Nell's hibiscus blossoms for dominance in the bed nearest the center of the yard. Several months went by. Nell rarely spent time among the flowers, or if she did, she showed up at odd times.

Real Worlds

Then one morning, as I walked past her house, a moving van pulled up to block the driveway. For several months, the house sat vacant. The untended beds grew out of control, lush with the summer rain. A dry snap at the beginning of August tortured the lawn into strands of rafia, and Nell's garden withered and shriveled in the blasting sun. Early in September, stacks of cardboard boxes with moving van labels appeared in the driveway, on the sidewalk and on top of flower beds. Nell and her handiwork disappeared. A few dry stalks of rosebushes and clumps of dried stems in frazzled heaps dotted the lawn.

The winter came and went. The house seemed inhabited by ghosts. Then one spring morning, an entire family knelt on the grass, chopping out dead plants, weeding, and staking straggly branches. Over the summer, Nell's garden enjoyed a rebirth. Without Nell's sure hand, pansies planted in the wrong exposure died, and a rose bush grew frosty with mildew. But bit by bit, many of Nell's plants came back to life. Once again the garden was beautiful.

Life is like Nell's garden. We plan and plant, nurture and nourish, and one day we move on. Some of what we've planted has hearty roots and grows deep. It will go on without us. Some of what we've planted will wither away as soon as we turn our backs. But we hope to leave behind a piece of beauty, some small improvement, that marks our time on this planet.

Real Worlds

This spring I planted geraniums and an annual garden behind my office. A friend was curious and asked, "Why did you go through all that effort? Aren't you moving to England? It's not like you'll be around to enjoy your work."

She's right. I won't be here, but another woman will be. She'll move into my house and enjoy the flowers I've left behind. I hope that across the ocean another woman is planting flowers in front of a house that I'll rent starting this midsummer. So it goes. We plant not only for ourselves, but also for those who come behind us.

P.S. That's exactly the way it happened, but the "woman" who planted my flowers is actually a very sweet gentleman named Jesus (pronounced "Hey-Seuss"). In fact, he's outside my window adding more flowers right now.

Real Worlds

BLESSING

*I want to leave the world a little better than
I found it. Let me focus on what I can
contribute, but remind me that
ultimately my legacy is your decision.*

1) *What can I leave behind as my legacy?*

_____
_____
_____

2) *List ways that others have made contributions to your life.*

_____
_____
_____
_____
_____

3) *Think of a new way you might make a contribution. What
would be your first step?*

_____
_____
_____
_____

4) *Tell someone how he or she has made your world a better
place.*

Nurture Yourself

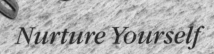

Nurture Yourself

You're Out
Too Far

I can still see her in my mind's eye although she's been gone for twenty years. I called her, "Gar Gar." She was my maternal grandmother.

She lived on Central Avenue in Summerville, South Carolina, in a house that her father had built from handpicked cypress wood. A house designed, like others, to offer wealthy families respite from the perils of malaria and other diseases that threatened the city of Charleston every summer.

Each year my mother would load us into the car before the sun came up, and we would make the long, long drive from Vincennes, Indiana, to Summerville. Along the way were many adventures: busted radiators, attacks by sweat bees in a rest stop and perilous views off the side of the mountain as we wound our way through Chattanooga. But the angels flew along with us, and eventually we'd pull into the sandy driveway behind the red-roofed, gabled house.

Keeping us busy for a month was a challenge. Fortunately for my mother, I was a reader and my sisters had friends nearby. The high points of our summer visits were the infrequent treks we'd make to the beach. These were treks that were always a full-day's ordeal, that included an hour's drive there and a sun-burned, sand-itching tortuous hour back.

Nurture Yourself

Once on the beach, my grandmother would open a folding lawn chair on the boardwalk or the sand. Her posture never varied. One hand held an Ellery Queen novel, its cover graced with a damsel in duress and undress. The other hand covered her eyes along with the clip-on sun visors she wore on her glasses. Each year she splurged on a new pair of "shades" from Izzy Kramer's Rexall Drugs.

On her feet were navy blue Keds with holes cut out of the toe box to make room for the cotton padding and tape which swathed her toes that had been crushed in a car accident. A battered straw hat kept slipping down the back of her head.

Janie and I would run and play in the waves. Sometimes we'd body-surf, throwing ourselves toward the beach and riding the water 'til we spilled on the sand. The undercurrent pulled us gently and imperceptibly farther and farther out. As we played, we lost our bearings and forgot to stay close to the strip mall that bordered Folly Beach.

So every once in a while, Gar Gar would rise up from her chair and cup her hands around her mouth to yell, "Sugar! Sugar! You are out too far!"

She would holler 'til we heard her. The sound was faint across the majesty of the water. Her arms would beat the sky for our attention.

With great effort, we would put our feet down on the sand. The sea would fight us for our balance, and often we would stand

Nurture Yourself

up only to tumble over and have to start again. Somehow, the water seemed a living thing, a deadly mother whose arms fought to hold us close. But, with an eye on Gar Gar, we'd ignore the roiling, roller coaster of foam behind us. We make our ears numb to the shrieks of laughter from other fun-seekers. We knew better than to compare ourselves to the other children and their parents who had ventured out so much farther than we ever dared.

"Stupid Yankees," she'd sputter with disgust as she'd dry us off with rough caresses of her towel.

"Look at 'em. Out so far. The undertow will get 'em. They think they're so smart."

She had reason to fuss. Many years before, her younger sister had lost a boyfriend to the current, and his body washed up on a deserted stretch of Carolina beaches. Gar Gar never repeated the story to us but then again, she didn't need to.

It occurs to me now, that we took very little responsibility for how deep we went into the water or how far the current carried us away. Gar Gar did that for us.

Today, I also go through times when I take little responsibility for my health, my time and my schedule. I allow myself to become too swept away by the currents of other people's demands. I forget I have the option of walking away—at least for a while, until I get back my balance. At these times, if I listen very carefully, I can hear a voice inside me calling, "Sugar! Sugar! You're out too far!"

Nurture Yourself

BLESSING

*Within each of us is a voice that tells us
when we are "out too far." Help me to
listen for it!*

*1) When was the last time you were out too far? What were
the signs?*

_____

_____

_____

_____

*2) Who in your life could help guide you back to the safety of
the sand?*

_____

_____

_____

_____

*3) Make for yourself a list of situations that have a tendency to
pull you insidiously, like the current. How can you pull yourself
back into balance?*

_____

_____

_____

_____

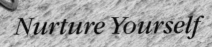

Nurture Yourself

Comfort Me

As our ceiling fan made lazy circles overhead, I ran through the list of what I had to do before our trans-Atlantic move. My mind jumped from task to task when suddenly a word blinked before my eyes like a flashing neon sign: FREEZER. I hadn't considered that the freezer would have to be emptied and defrosted before the movers could haul it out for storage.

Early the next morning, I started to sift through the food we'd collected. Fortunately, the frozen Lean Cuisines and Weight Watchers would be snapped up quickly by my convenience-loving family. Then I dug a little deeper and uncovered row after row of homemade soup.

Stacked two high on a cookie sheet, I transported the frozen soups to my sink. After the hot water secured the soup's release, I let them sit in the sink over the garbage disposal to defrost. In about an hour's time, my sink was an inch deep with groady goop.

"Yuck," said Michael. "That's so gross, Mom." He was right. While I rinsed defrosted pieces down the disposal, I chastised myself. Whatever was I thinking? How could one person have frozen all this food? My husband and son don't even like my homemade soup. Was I crazy?

Nurture Yourself

Beating yourself up sends your energy level into a steep decline. My "to do" list now seemed impossible to conquer. Feeling wasteful, I washed the stacked up freezer containers. Children are starving in Africa, and I'm freezing soup by the bucket. What a world, what a world. Finally feeling totally paralyzed, I grabbed my shoes and went for a long walk. Two miles down the road and two miles uphill back. Now the sink looked different to me.

I'd made the soup because I find soup comforting. Smelling soup on the stove while I write makes me feel rich on the deepest levels. After all, I'm being creative both in the abstract and in the solid worlds. Much of what I write never sees print. I've learned to live with that waste. When you write, you need to turn on your creative faucet and let it flow. With the editing process, you selectively cull out the waste. It's a lot like making soup. It's nearly impossible to make one cup of soup that tastes good. You make a pot of soup and dip out a cup or a bowl to eat.

Once the connection was made between comfort and making soup, I realized it wasn't entirely wasteful. By making the soup, I had offered myself comfort. My plan had been to re-heat the extra, but it just didn't work out. If more of us took responsibility for comforting ourselves, we could be kinder to each other. If the cost of kindness is three cups of soup, so be it.

Nurture Yourself

BLESSING

*I can comfort and nurture myself. Once I
learn to comfort myself, I can reach out to
others. When I do this, the world becomes a
better place.*

1) How do you comfort yourself?

_____

_____

_____

_____

*2) Think of what comforted you as a child. Can you make that
part of your life today?*

_____

_____

_____

_____

*3) How can you bring an air of contentment into your family life?
Your life at work? Your time spent with friends?*

_____

_____

_____

_____

_____

Callaway's Rule

Ely Callaway changed the game of golf forever when he created clubs that hit the ball farther with less muscle and skill. The United States Golf Association recognizes a mere 34 rules but you don't have to be a golfer to appreciate Ely Callaway's greatest contribution to the game, Rule 35: Have fun.

I think Callaway could have been talking to parents.

We are champion worriers. We fret and we fuss. How easy it is to overlook the fact that childhood should be fun, both for parents and for kids.

When I ask my son to think of our best times together, he always rehashes our unplanned, spontaneous times of fun. Here's a partial list:

1. **Going on toad walks.** After 10 p.m., we grab a flashlight and wander down the streets of our subdivision spotting toads. We keep track on our garage wall of how many we see. The record was 14 in one night.

2. **Driving to Grandma Marge's.** By taking the scenic route, we could choose from five to six Wal-Marts along the way. When Michael grew restless, we'd pull into a parking lot, buy

a snack and stop to try his skill at a "claw" machine, where he could grab for toys.

3. **Lighting sparklers**. I waited until he was eleven because I worried about safety. Michael was fascinated by the trail a moving sparkler could leave as you waved your arm in a lazy figure eight.

4. **Watching movies**. During the most forbidding weather of winter, we'd pop popcorn, drag blankets down from the upstairs bedrooms and watch movies while sitting side by side on the sofa.

5. **Playing four square**. His favorite game is one I really stink at. Watching a parent fail BIG TIME is such fun for a kid. All of us parents need our egos adjusted on a regular basis.

6. **Going exploring**. Michael loves to wander around the lakes in our subdivision. He's caught snapping turtles, sliders, frogs, box turtles, fish, crawdads, and a bullfrog. I hope he never overcomes his reticence about grabbing snakes. He has just the right amount of caution, and I pray it stays with him.

Last Christmas, we didn't get around to building a gingerbread house. Mid-February, I decided the house could be a love shack, after the funky song by the same name. I bought candy-hearts, red licorice, gum drops and conversation hearts. One evening after Joon Ho, our Korean exchange student, finished his session with Mihye, his tutor, we all worked to decorate

Nurture Yourself

our love shack. The white icing was perfectly gooey. We stuck candies all around the building. Then we decorated the tin foil platform I'd made as a landscape for the house. We giggled non-stop for nearly an hour.

When the time came to clean up, because we were out of icing and candy, Mihye became pensive. "This was such fun," she said. "Right now there is only me and my husband. We would never have done this."

Smart woman. Without giving birth, she's stumbled onto one of the great secrets of parenthood: When you have kids, you automatically grant yourself permission to do silly stuff. The boys didn't care about the love shack, but I did. Without their presence, the effort seemed wasteful. It wasn't.

Callaway understood our need to play. We don't need our children to give us an excuse.

Nurture Yourself

BLESSING

As I look around the world, I notice the playfulness inherent in all nature. Let me always have a playful place in my heart.

1) *What would the kid in you like to do?*

_____

_____

_____

_____

_____

2) *What's stopping you?*

_____

_____

_____

_____

_____

_____

3) *Commit to doing something playful, however small, every day.*

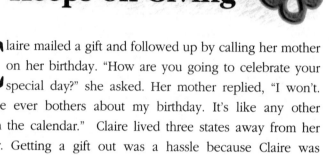

Nurture Yourself

Guilt: The Gift that Keeps on Giving

Claire mailed a gift and followed up by calling her mother on her birthday. "How are you going to celebrate your special day?" she asked. Her mother replied, "I won't. No one ever bothers about my birthday. It's like any other day on the calendar." Claire lived three states away from her mother. Getting a gift out was a hassle because Claire was getting her son ready to go off to college and her husband had been out-of-town. Feeling guilty, she hung up the phone. Then, her son yelled from his room upstairs, "Mom, did you finish sewing the buttons on my good shirt?"

Robert's father sighed over his meal. "I guess you and Mary aren't going to have kids," Robert's dad bowed his gray head low over the plate. "The family name will die out. Such a shame. I was counting on being a grandparent." Stunned, Robert somehow got out of the restaurant. Recounting the conversation with his wife, she reminded him that he had three male cousins, two male second cousins and a brother with the same last name. Robert still felt sick about letting his father down.

Nurture Yourself

Margie Sommers' daughter had recently broken up with a guy who had "potential." On the spur of the moment, Margie flew to Sacramento to spend a few days with her daughter. She and Lynnie had burgers at In and Out, went shopping and talked about the future. Two days after Margie returned home, her mother-in-law phoned. When she discovered that Margie and Lynnie were within driving distance of her home in Reno, she pitched a fit. "Both of you are disrespectful," boomed Mrs. Sommers. "You could have taken me to lunch or dinner. You know how lonely I am." Mrs. Sommers complained about the situation to her son, so Len Sommers was forced to quiz his wife, "Couldn't you have at least dropped by? Or called Mom?"

No matter how much some of us do, we could always do more for our family. Sociologists call us Baby Boomers, the sandwich generation because we are squeezed here in the middle. You, me and the bologna. By taking care of one generation, we upset another generation. So, we are not only in the middle, but we're usually there alone. Forget the bologna analogy. Actually, we're more like mozzarella cheese, because when life heats up, we get spread thin, stretch and eventually we snap.

Nurture Yourself

What helps?

1. **A sympathetic ear**. A friend who's been there and who knows you need to vent.

2. **A reality check**. No one knows what you are juggling but you. Remember, others see only a snapshot of our lives. We are all ignorant of each other to a degree. If they could see all you do, all the stresses you weather, your family members would respond differently.

3. **A mantra**. Repeat to yourself: I'm doing the best I can. Then take a deep breath.

Nurture Yourself

BLESSING

Let me appreciate that other people need me.
While it may seem like a burden, it's also a
sign that I have worth. Guide me to listen to my
own needs so I can then be of service to others.

1) What triggers your guilt?

_____

_____

_____

2) Who offers a sympathetic ear?

_____

_____

_____

3) Who offers a reality check?

_____

_____

_____

4) How can you give yourself a reality check? Find an affirmation
that works for you.

_____

_____

_____

_____

Nurture Yourself

What Makes You Happy?

A friend of mine who is a therapist gives a very, very simple test for depression. He asks, "What makes you happy?" If the respondent can't come up with any answers, the therapist knows to check further for depression.

In the bleak days of February, when piles of dirty snow edge the streets and melted spots uncover collections of grubby trash, we need to work to focus on happiness. I strain when I try to look past the dull brown of the tree branches and think about spring when the trees blush with color-green, rose, red and yellow. But since spring seems so far away, I am brought back again to the question, "What makes me happy?"

The answer, I think, would make a great scrapbook page. I would list:

- ❑ Curling up with my dog on the sofa as I read a book
- ❑ Butterscotch candies
- ❑ "You've got mail!" on my computer
- ❑ Warm pajamas on a cold night
- ❑ Hearing my car start right up!
- ❑ Seeing my son's smile
- ❑ A hot pot of soup bubbling in the crock pot
- ❑ The fragrance of my lavender body lotion

Nurture Yourself

- ❑ A phone message that a friend has had her baby
- ❑ Watching birds come to our feeder
- ❑ Helping my son win a stuffed animal from an arcade
- ❑ Sipping hot tea from my mug with violets on it
- ❑ Opening a freshly developed pack of photos
- ❑ Getting scrapbook pages finished for my upcoming book
- ❑ Wrapping my grandmother's quilt around me at night
- ❑ Finally doing The Crow pose in yoga for a split second
- ❑ Having pink polish on my toenails
- ❑ Lighting the candles on Friday nights
- ❑ Hearing my friend's voice on the phone
- ❑ Using Caller I.D. to ignore a telemarketer
- ❑ Discovering a $10 bill in my jeans pocket
- ❑ Visiting the little grocery store in my village (the floors are sloping and made of wood, the owner's doll collection lines the top shelf, the clerks write our purchases down in a little notepad and bill us)
- ❑ Hugging a friend, my son's teacher, after hearing her surgery went well

And Michael, who's home today with a slight fever left over from a bout with the stomach flu, adds his own list:

- ❑ Writing books with my mom
- ❑ Playing baseball with my dad

Nurture Yourself

- ❏ Playing computer with Joon Ho
- ❏ Watching Kevin (our dog) do silly things like thinking it over before he jumps up on the sofa

Have you considered how you would answer? I hope you are inspired to create your own list. Focusing on the good in life may not come naturally at first, but with a smidge of practice, you'll find it a habit worth cultivating.

Nurture Yourself

BLESSING

Help me pay more attention to all the daily joys in my life.

1) What's on your happiness list?

_____

_____

_____

_____

2) When's the last time you did something that made you happy?

_____

_____

_____

3) How could you add happiness to another person's day?

_____

_____

_____

5) Who helps you to be happy? Can you spend more time with that person?

_____

_____

_____

_____

Nurture Yourself

Be Reasonfull

Y ou read that right. Moms must be reasonfull so that our families support us in all our endeavors.

For example, when Michael was only three, he puckered up his face on the way home from day care and asked me why some mothers came to pick up his classmates at noon and why I didn't show up until after snack. He had caught on to the idea that I was "missing in action." With that inquiry, he was introduced to his mother, the working woman.

To a child, a working mom is often an abstract idea. After all, what do you do? And why? If you can take your child to where you work, he might realize that others depend on what you do when you are away from home. If you work out of your home, explaining your "other job" is trickier. To Michael, there was no "reason" that I couldn't stop work earlier in the day.

Shortly afterwards, I had an idea. Michael's pre-school was within walking distance of a McDonald's. Once a week as I dropped Michael off in the morning, I'd also leave behind his stroller. In the afternoon, I'd walk to Michael's school, put him in the stroller, and we'd head for McDonald's. After a snack, we'd catch a city bus that ran within a mile of our house. Then I'd push him home in the stroller. This routine

Nurture Yourself

satisfied my need for exercise, and Michael's love of french fries and buses.

My idea was to link the treats we enjoyed at McDonald's with my work. On our next weekly visit to Mickey D's, I handed Michael a few bills to hold. "This is the money I earned from writing books," I said. "It's book money." After he paid for our food, I reminded him again that we were eating with "book money."

After a couple more visits, Michael seemed to understand that my work paved the way for his enjoyment. I gave him a reason for my being an "afternoon pick up" mother. Of course, as he has gotten older, I've been able to explain that writing is what I love to do. He now accepts my work as a part of me. And yes, there are times he thinks I work too much, but that's understandable.

A recent study by Ohio State University found that men were more likely to be active if they had support from their friends, and women were more likely to exercise if their families encouraged them. Hence, women need to be more reasonfull. We need to point out to our families the reasons they should support us whether we are exercising, taking time for ourselves or working outside the home. When we are reasonfull, our entire family stands to benefit.

Nurture Yourself

BLESSING

*Instead of working against others who
love me, give me the tools to
enlighten them.*

1) *In what area of life do you need more understanding from
your family?*

_____
_____
_____

2) *How does taking care of yourself help your family?*

_____
_____
_____

3) *Do you even admit that you need your family's support? Why
or why not?*

_____
_____

4) *What is the role of a family? Do you see a family as a group of
people bound by love and the commitment to support each other?
If not, how would you describe a family?*

_____
_____
_____

Taking Charge

Taking Charge

In The No Phone Zone

"May I speak to Janet?" I asked. The voice on the other end of the line snapped, "This is Jan." I burst out laughing. "Calm down, kiddo."

You have to know her to understand that this exchange is entirely out of character. Jan giggles at least twice each sentence. Many times I've wished God had granted me her sunny disposition. To be growled at by Jan is unthinkable. She had even surprised herself.

"Thanks for knowing that's not really me," she said. "I've had eight calls from phone solicitors in a row, and I guess I lost it."

So often other people work on us the way an icicle forms off the edge of a gutter. A drip, drip, drip builds up and then we crack. Undesirable calls from phone solicitors interrupt our lives. The worst offenders pretend to be our friends, calling us cheerily by our first names. A few refuse to take no for an answer. One even called me back immediately to suggest I couldn't hang up until I had heard his entire pitch.

With e-mail, faxes and phone calls, we are never alone. Our solitude must compete with our culture's demand that we are available 24/7. For women, the problem is compounded by

Taking Charge

our natural desire to remain accessible to those who love and need us. Each time I hesitate to answer the phone, I wonder if the Caller I.D. is displaying a phone booth or a borrowed cell phone. What if? I wonder. What if my son has borrowed another parent's cell phone to call me? What if my niece is calling me from a pay phone because she's at the mall and needs to talk to me privately? What if that call from out-of-the-area is my aunt on one of her travels?

I pick up the phone expecting to hear the voice of a person who matters. I am bushwhacked by a marketer's agenda. I feel like I've been tricked, and I have been. I respond to the next call with a cynical greeting or just as Jan did, with a growl of dismay.

But that's not really me. Only I can decide who I am and how I will respond to the demands of the world. After Jan and I hang up, I make myself a pledge to answer the phone with my best self. If I don't, the solicitors have taken more than my time and privacy; they've stolen my sense of perspective.

Taking Charge

BLESSING

I am in control of my reactions. No one can force me to change my attitude. Keep me resolute and balanced.

1) What is your attitude when you answer the phone?

_____

_____

_____

2) Is there a standard line you can use to politely get rid of unwanted calls?

_____

_____

_____

_____

3) How can you regain your equilibrium when you feel your privacy has been invaded?

_____

_____

_____

TIP: Consider establishing an "incommunicado" zone, a time where you are not available to any outside requests. In this way, you can preserve your energy for what is important to you.

Taking Charge

Why We Unplugged the TV

Every morning our family wound up fighting over the TV. Michael would bounce out of bed, turn on the set in our bedroom and become totally engrossed. It didn't matter that David and I might still be sleeping. It didn't matter that he was too old for Barney or too young for Good Morning America. Then he would sit like a zombie while we yelled, threatened and manipulated his limbs to put on his clothes.

If food was in front of him, he might take a tentative bite or two. But otherwise, he was oblivious to all that happened to him. Most mornings, our dog Kevin would snatch Michael's breakfast just as Michael glanced down at the plate. Then, Michael would scream and swat at Kevin, Kevin would yelp and run between my legs, and David would growl about germs.

Each morning ended with us hauling a protesting child into the car to go to pre-school. For the first fifteen minutes thereafter, anger and frustration reigned. Often, I would return home wanting only to crawl into bed and sob.

Sounds pretty dumb, doesn't it? It was. Why I took so long to change the situation, I'll never understand—except to say in my defense, I, too, was enchanted by the television. I was easily engrossed. For better or worse, I live much of my life

Taking Charge

in my head. So, I understood that Michael was not trying to be difficult. I knew he was mesmerized. He really didn't hear us, and his protests were born out of his frustration, not out of disobedience.

Once I looked at the situation objectively, there was a simple solution. We turned off the TV. We said, "No TV in the morning before school."

Wow! That little black box had heap powerful medicine. Just disconnecting its tentacles from our son in the morning made a tremendous difference. Mornings began to progress smoothly after that. Sure, there were a few fussy times, but the number of those was negligible when compared to what had been our daily ration.

David and I then began to discuss canceling cable altogether, which was a bold move because without cable we would have no reception. Without reception, our TV could only function as a big screen for the VCR and the Nintendo game.

We debated the pros and cons. We looked at the price we paid for cable and discussed the availability of video tapes. Then we took the plunge.

Our decision came at the start of the summer. All summer long, we replaced our TV time with other activities. The list follows:

Taking Charge

- ❑ Michael and I caught four toads
- ❑ Michael and I caught grasshoppers to feed the toads
- ❑ Michael and I went for walks
- ❑ David and Michael played ball
- ❑ David and Michael played Nintendo
- ❑ We all played Uno
- ❑ Michael played educational computer games to improve his math, reading and science skills
- ❑ Michael and I went to the library
- ❑ Michael read forty books and qualified for reading awards
- ❑ We all went to the neighborhood pool
- ❑ We all pitched in to make dinner, and we all pitched in to clean up afterwards
- ❑ We had family movie nights where we would all sit down together and watch a movie on the VCR

By the end of the summer, we were convinced: TV had rotted our brains. Like any addicts, we had ignored the growing hold television had over us. Only as the effects of the drug wore off, did we recapture our time together as a family. We actually began to have conversations at the dinner table, instead of dragging our meals over to the coffee table in front of the TV and sitting in silence.

David put it best. "Before we turned off the TV, the most we said to each other was, 'Move, you're in my way.'"

Taking Charge

Besides getting to know each other, we noticed other benefits. Michael quit demanding toys. Without television to fuel his acquisition lust, he learned to enjoy what he already had.

Michael's reading and math skills improved so much that after two weeks in kindergarten, the school called us and asked to move him into first grade.

Last but far from least, Michael calmed down considerably. After watching cartoons, he would often kick at the dog. Of course, we would discipline him, but he would still act like a Power Ranger on a regular basis. Even when he watched shows that were recommended for kids, the commercials would set him off.

Now when people tell me they don't have time to read or that their family never talks, I ask, "How much TV do you watch?" The number of hours reported astounds me. And it worries me.

Want a better life for your family? Pull the plug on the brain drug. If you're too chicken to go cold turkey, try this: No TV on weekday nights. Videotape the shows you would like to see and view them on the weekend. (Thanks for the great idea, Ross and Connie Ament and boys!)

If it's not worth the effort to tape, it wasn't worth your time to watch.

Taking Charge

BLESSING

*I am in control of my life. I can choose
much of what I want to see and hear.
I can choose what affects me.*

*1) Note your family's behavior patterns around the TV, the radio,
the movies. Note how you feel after watching the news on TV.*

_____

_____

_____

_____

*2) Write down what happens when you do not get to watch TV for
an evening or during a weekend away.*

_____

_____

_____

_____

*3) Now decide how much influence you want the media to have
on your family's life. Make a plan.*

_____

_____

_____

_____

Taking Charge

Wash Your Car

The cab driver had promised to pick us up, but there we were, standing on the street, miles away from our hotel in downtown Memphis. David and I must have looked a tad forlorn when the owner checked on us.

"Cab hasn't come?" he asked. To our negative response, he shook his head and scuffed his foot. Then he hurried back inside the concrete block building. Moments later he reappeared with three women walking beside him. "She'll take you to the Peabody," he called, pointing to one woman and using his hands as a megaphone. Without hesitation, we raced across the street to follow the ladies.

"Now don't look at my car," protested the driver. The back seat was littered with programs from the AME church she attended. The other two ladies, members of Link who had come to Memphis for their annual convention, piled in along side us. "Really," said our driver as she turned to her full backseat, "Please forgive the mess in this car," and she went on to apologize for several more minutes.

When she took a break, I interjected, "You know, the specific reason I came to the restaurant today was to inspect the quality of cleanliness in local cars." A quick pause followed and then, we all laughed. Here this kind woman was transporting four

Taking Charge

people she'd never met, and she was thinking we were hung up on the junk in her car.

Still, I understand where she was coming from. I'm convinced that my car runs better when it's clean.

Watching the brushes scrub away dirt and grime is positively therapeutic. Seeing that big vacuum suck up crumbs, dirt balls, and candy wrappers gives me a thrill. When I sorely need a laugh, I take my convertible through the drive-through car wash. Even with the top and windows up, a few streams of water always manage to squirt through. As I play dodge the deluge, I have to laugh.

Call me sick. Say I'm demented. I don't care. All of us Americans seem to have symbiotic relationships with our wheels.

After all, my car functions as my home away from home. In the summer, I fill a jelly jar with marbles, flowers and water and put it in the cup holder. When I travel, I stock up on books on tape and recordings from my favorite motivators. I always find Chex mix or popcorn snack cakes in the glove compartment to munch on.

One day I took my neighbor and her daughter to an exhibit at a mall. No sooner had they hopped into the car when the child said, "Mom! Look how clean her car is!" I hit a mental high beam.

The next time you feel low, head for the car wash. Or make up your mind not to let that messy car ruin your day.

Taking Charge

BLESSING

*Order around us improves our sense of
order within us. Let us strive to create
pleasant environments, but keep us
focused on what really matters, our
relationships with other people.*

*1) How clean is your car right now? Does having a tidy car
matter to you?*

_____

_____

_____

_____

*2) Have you ever turned away from an opportunity because you
felt your car or your home or your person wasn't presentable?*

_____

_____

_____

_____

3) Create an affirmation to focus on what is really important.

_____

_____

_____

_____

Taking Charge

What I Like Best

As the thermometer climbs outside, domestic violence and other forms of assault take a corresponding climb upwards. Determined to prove the temperature/violence correlation, the two eleven-year-olds in the backseat were grabbing Game Boys out of each other's hands. After spending the morning on boogie boards at the beach, my son Michael and his pal Kip were toasted to a rosy pink on their shoulders and noses. We had only been cooped up in the hot car for about fifteen minutes as we waited for my husband to pick up a fax from the business office at Kiawah Island, but it felt like a life sentence in a Moroccan desert jail. Suddenly, our splendid idea of bringing one of Michael's friends with us on a family vacation seemed stupid. Of course, the boys were bound to grow tired of each other. Of course, they would fight. Whatever were we thinking?

"We are going to play a game," I announced, turning around from the front passenger seat. My husband slid into the driver's seat as I asserted my parental command posture. "The game," I continued although their attention was half-hearted, "is called 'What I Liked Best.' Each of us will take turns saying one thing we've liked best about this vacation. David, will you go first?"

Taking Charge

My husband seemed to sense my unspoken cry for help. "What I liked best about this vacation has been listening to The Breeze, the radio station that plays beach, boogie and blues. I especially like it because we can't get it at home."

I jumped in. "I liked the smell of the pines best. The smell of South Carolina always makes me happy" and with that, I turned expectantly to Michael.

He frowned. Then Kip spoke up, "I liked crabbing the best. Man, that was cool."

Not to be outdone, Michael added, "I liked that baby turtle we found on the seashore. He was so cute."

Soon, the guys were outdoing themselves competing to think of the good times we'd had, and the sites we'd enjoyed. The mood lightened. For the next few days of the vacation, we trotted out the "What I Like Best" game for numerous repeat performances.

Taking Charge

BLESSING

Teach me the art of positive focus.
Encourage me to turn my energies toward
appreciating all life's gifts. Remind me that I
can always choose where to direct my attention.

1) Create a list of positive focus sentences such as "What I Liked Best" and "My Favorite Thing Is…"

_____

_____

_____

_____

_____

_____

_____

2) For at least a week, list only good times, feelings and thoughts at the end of each day. Get into the habit of being grateful for the good.

_____

_____

_____

_____

_____

_____

_____

Taking Charge

3) Think of a person in your life who seems to have mastered positive focus. How do you feel when you are around that person?

_____

_____

_____

_____

_____

_____

_____

4) Revisit an old and difficult situation. What positives can you now see as a result of that situation?

_____

_____

_____

_____

_____

_____

_____

Taking Charge

When All Else Fails

" It's me. Olivia. Mom took a fall. I'm on my way to Austin to figure out what to do. I won't be there Thursday. I'll have to wait and call to let you know what's up," and with that, Olivia said goodbye.

When you are friends, and you know about each other's lives, you can say so much in a few words. Although Olivia's call took less than thirty seconds, she'd packed in a lifetime of information by implication. She'd managed to tell me she was worried. Clearly, she was nervous. Her hands would be full. Since her mother suffered from severe allergies, moving her to assisted living was out of the question. One errant visitor wearing perfumes, or one unaware custodian spraying disinfectant could send Mrs. Smith into a painful allergic reaction. As an only child, Olivia was forced to be the one to make important choices about her mother's welfare. For better or worse, no committee of siblings would back her up or challenge her decisions.

And there seemed to be no way to help my friend.

Oh, I could dig up Olivia's cell phone number and call her. But, did she really need an interruption?

Taking Charge

Suddenly, I felt helpless and restive all at once. I wanted to help. I didn't want to intrude. I wanted to lend Olivia my strength.

So I lit a candle. As the match flame caught hold, I imagined myself reflected in one of those infinity mirrors. My hand trembling over the wick, holding the fire, would go on and on and on. This was a candle for Olivia, for her mother, for another friend whose daughter is severely brain-damaged, for my sister recovering from her Cesarean, for my mother's recent surgery, for our upcoming move, for Amy who lives in war-torn Israel with two small daughters, for the family dealing with a daughter's estrangement, for Elaine's move to a new home, and on and on.

An old saying came back to me: "Don't tell God how big your problems are. Tell your problems how big God is."

Taking Charge

BLESSING

Let us learn to have faith in the greater power of the universe. There is no problem or situation that God cannot handle.

1) Create a list of people or situations you might pray for.

_____

_____

_____

_____

_____

_____

_____

2) Find a quiet space and light a candle. Let the stillness comfort you. How do you feel?

_____

_____

_____

_____

_____

_____

_____

Taking Charge

3) Consider your feelings about a Higher Power. How can you put your trust in that higher power.

_____

_____

_____

_____

_____

_____

_____

Taking Charge

Pockets of Joy

A t one point in my career as a motivational speaker, I was traveling two or three times a month. Inevitably, the women in my audiences would say, "How exciting!" Inevitably, I'd sigh and tell myself, "How exciting."

The truth is there are only so many little soaps you can take before the novelty of hotels wears thin. Having someone clean your room and make your bed is fine, but honestly, I could have made the bed myself and the bathroom didn't get that messy overnight.

Yes, I'd earned frequent flyer points and could have flown first class, but folks, there is no first class in crop dusters unless you want to sit on the pilot's lap. Since the pilot often looked too young to drive a car much less fly a plane, I was happy to sit in the back and not be a distraction.

I do love to travel, but I also missed my family, my home and my dog. Clients came in all shapes and sizes and temperaments. A few spoiled me shamelessly, welcoming me with baskets of goodies and taking me out to eat. Others sent me to dubious lodging where my room on the ground floor was easily accessible to all predators, and the lack of room service meant I made a meal from instant soup and whatever I could punch out of the vending machines.

Taking Charge

One day, feeling particularly lonely, I called home. David was in a hurry to get off the phone so he and Michael could go to a movie. Michael was already out the door and waiting in the car. I dressed to give my speech in silence, feeling awfully sorry for myself. Here I was alone, soon to meet 500 people whom I hoped to charm and entertain. I sure didn't feel charming or entertaining. I gave myself a once-over and slipped on my jacket. In the pocket was a lump. That lump was a tiny toy airplane my son had given me to hold a few days before.

I grinned. Hey, I'd be home soon. My kid would be waiting to see what I'd brought him. My husband and I would snuggle together at night. I was alone, temporarily, but no longer lonely.

The presentation went well, in part due to my good mood. As I spoke, I'd slip my hand into my pocket and touch the little plane like a talisman. The incident took on mythical proportions in my mind as I mentally named it my "pocket of joy."

Since then, whenever I travel I build in a pocket of joy. I plan for a treat or special experience, whether it's getting to read a good book that I've been saving or showering with a new bath product. Rather than leave my happiness to chance, I actively create joy. You'd be amazed at what a difference it makes to take control of your moods.

Oh, and I never clean my pockets out if I can help it. What stays in them from season to season and wearing to wearing is meant to be. In this situation, my messiness blesses me.

Taking Charge

BLESSING

I can nurture myself. Show me ways to take more responsibility for my own pleasures. Direct me to assertively take charge of my moods. Help me practice self-reliance.

1) List a few talismans you own. Do you carry any of them with you?

_____

_____

_____

_____

2) Why do these particular possessions make you happy?

_____

_____

_____

_____

3) Make a list of happy thoughts. Put this list in your wallet with your money so that you can frequently remind yourself of where your true wealth comes from. Put a few lists of happy thoughts in the pockets of clothes that you won't be wearing right away.

_____

_____

_____

_____

Bonus

Bonus

The Four Basic Food Groups

by Jan Breyer

We've taken the opportunity to share with you the work of a new, unpublished writer. Enjoy!

I don't know how babies manage to surprise us when we have nearly nine months to prepare, but they do. When I heard the news of Leandra's arrival, I wished for a few more days to get a gift ready for Danielle's little girl.

Despite the fact the pretty gift bag had sat on my dining room table for weeks, it still lacked something, something special. I yearned for a magic moment of Martha Stewart inspiration.

Danielle's baby deserved special something—a gift that was a blessing to both mother and child. A gift to repay Danielle for her kindness to my twin boys.

Years ago, I had learned the hard way that when you are moving to a new town, the best you can hope for is a real estate agent who tolerates kids. Danielle, although childless herself at the time, exceeded my expectations by completely understanding kids. I watched in amazement as she handed both my boys a goody bag to keep them occupied during the

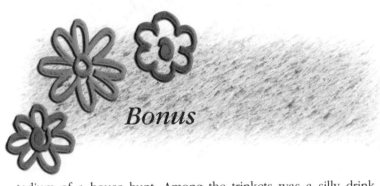

Bonus

tedium of a house hunt. Among the trinkets was a silly drink with tiny ball-like bubbles suspended in the goo. How did she know my sons would love that? Had she been standing behind us when I had previously refused to buy this concoction?

Danielle laughed. "That drink seemed like it covered the four basic food groups for boys—sugary, gross, green and wiggly."

Curiously when we found a house, Danielle went from being our agent to our neighbor. Yet, her kindness to our sons never waned. Obviously, her interest in children was not merely a marketing gimmick. The gift bag on the table called out to me to repay her kindness. But what was missing? On my work table were leftover beads from my last jewelry project. I scooted the letters this way and that. There was an L, N, A, R, D and yes, even an E! Quickly I strung the bracelet finishing off LEANDRA in beads with a delicate clasp. My gift was nearer perfection, but still not complete. I'd run out of time, though. I grabbed up the bag and reminded my husband of his offer to accompany me to the hospital.

As we stopped at the hospital information desk for directions to the maternity ward, he peered into the gift bag. "Gum balls, lip liner and a bracelet? I don't get the connection," he asked.

"Think of it as the four basic food groups for girls: candy, make up, jewelry, and ..." I stopped. That elusive missing article was now on the tip of my tongue.

"And?" prodded my husband.

Bonus

"And SHOES!" I shouted. Quickly veering into the gift shop, I raced up and down the aisles. I looked high and low. Finally, I accepted defeat. Turning to walk out, my coat brushed the top of a display table. Pausing to right whatever I had knocked asunder, I saw a pair of frilly white socks next to a shiny set of infant-sized black patent leather shoes.

"Come on, darlings," I said as I dangled the licorice-colored shoes before my husband's laughing eyes. "You've got a date with a sweet little girl."

Bonus

BLESSING

I am blessed to be able to give back to others. Help me to select gifts that send messages of love and appreciation.

1) What are the four basic food groups of your life?

_____
_____
_____
_____

2) What special gifts are on your list right now? Can you find items to fit a basic food group for someone special?

_____
_____
_____

3) Brainstorm some possible ideas for gifts.

_____
_____
_____
_____
_____
_____

Bonus

A Note from Home

My husband David has never been fond of our dog Kevin. David calls him, "Kevin the Wonder Dog. I wonder why I ever agreed to owning a dog."

I understand. David is a cat person. Cat people have trouble making the adjustment to a pet that is so exuberantly loving. David preferred his old cat Tinker, a walking advertisement for overbreeding at its worst. Tinker, a Siamese male, had crossed eyes, a kinked tail, a herniated abdomen which caused his stomach to drag along the floor, and such foul breath he could wake you out of a deep sleep just by breathing in your face. If he didn't get your attention by standing on your face, he'd yowl in your ear. Or, bite you. Definitely, a unique advertisement for his breed.

Yes, old Tinker was a piece of work, and a well-loved piece of work at that, until one sad day his misbegotten body finally lay down in our basement and died.

We needed a replacement pet. The house was too quiet.

Then, I found Kevin, a frisky Bichon Frise, who looked for all the world like a very happy little dust mop on legs. Too happy, it seemed, for poor David, who preferred pets who ignore him and make him sneeze.

Bonus

Obviously, taking Kevin to the groomer will never rank high on David's priority list. Still, delegating is one of the keys to good time management and I wasn't about to let a little whining stop me from getting the help I needed.

"But, hon! The groomer is on your way to work," I persisted. "It's silly for me to spend half an hour dropping him off when it's on your way."

David scowled. "Come on, dog-breath," and he set off for the car, with Kevin bouncing along beside him.

Fifteen minutes went by. The phone rang.

"Mrs. Slan? Your husband just showed up with Kevin, and, uh, we were wondering," the receptionist sounded very nervous. "Do you really want us to give Kevin a frontal lobotomy?"

I stomped back downstairs to my office. This meant war. My husband had just upped the ante, and I meant to get even.

I bided my time.

Six weeks passed. Kevin was once again a dirty shadow of his fluffy, fur ball self. His cute little blue hair bow hung from his topknot in tatters.

"Come on, David. Puhleeze. Take him to the groomer," I begged. Kevin sat on his bottom and pawed the air prettily.

David looked up from his coffee and snarled. "Okay, but this time I want you to write down exactly what you want them

Bonus

to do. I don't even want to have to discuss that mangy mutt with them. Understand?"

I smiled. "Of course, darling."

He tucked my note into the pocket of his suit coat and gave Kevin a yank. "Come on, you poor excuse for a poodle." And Kevin followed him joyously into the garage. As they pulled out of the driveway, David was hunkering over the steering wheel, while Kevin's black button eyes peered out the window, the blue bow bobbing up and down.

At the groomers, David stepped up to the counter with assurance. The receptionist cooed over Kevin. "What can we do for you today, Mr. Slan?"

David smiled his smug little grin and handed the lady the note I had written.

The receptionist began to laugh hysterically. Another groomer pulled the note from her hand and read it. Now two groomers were in stitches. David's smile was slipping.

"Could we hurry this along? I have to get to work," he snapped.

They laughed harder.

Finally, they showed him the note. I had printed my instructions very neatly: *Bathe the dog. Neuter the husband.*

Bonus

Blessing

Help me to see the gift, medicine and tool that humor is.

1) Think of a situation that irritates you. How could you add humor and lightness to uplift the situation?

_____

_____

_____

_____

2) How else can you plan to weave humor into tense situations? Think of a situation that always creates unrest in your household.

_____

_____

_____

_____

3) What makes you laugh? How do you feel when you have a really good laugh about something?

_____

_____

_____

_____

Bonus

BLESSINGS JOURNAL

_____
_____
_____
_____
_____
_____
_____
_____
_____
_____
_____
_____
_____
_____
_____
_____
_____
_____
_____
_____
_____
_____
_____
_____
_____
_____
_____
_____
_____

Bonus

BLESSINGS JOURNAL

_____
_____
_____
_____
_____
_____
_____
_____
_____
_____
_____
_____
_____
_____
_____
_____
_____
_____
_____
_____
_____
_____
_____
_____
_____
_____
_____
_____
_____
_____
_____
_____
_____

Bonus

BLESSINGS JOURNAL

Bonus

BLESSINGS JOURNAL

_____
_____
_____
_____
_____
_____
_____
_____
_____
_____
_____
_____
_____
_____
_____
_____
_____
_____
_____
_____
_____
_____
_____
_____
_____
_____
_____
_____
_____
_____
_____
_____
_____

Bonus

BLESSINGS JOURNAL

Bonus

BLESSINGS JOURNAL

Bonus

ISBN: 0-9630222-8-8
128 pages (1999) $19.⁹⁹

Scrapbook Storytelling

Save family stories and memories with photos, journaling and your own creativity.

Learn how to document stories—from a quick sentence to page after scrapbook page. This book is full of ways to recover stories from the past, discover the stories in the present and create stories that light the path to the future.

With easy to understand steps for journaling stories, readers can choose to combine narrative with photos, graphics, memorabilia and more.

ISBN: 0-930500-02-5
80 pages (2001) $14.⁹⁹

Quick & Easy Pages

Save more memories in less time.

If you've ever wished you had more time to scrapbook, or didn't think you had the time to start, this is the book for you. Joanna shares easy ways to present photographs and pull together pages. You'll learn over a hundred speedy scrapbooking techniques along with dozens of money-saving tips. Great how-to photos guide you through each step.

Bonus

ISBN: 0-930500-01-7
80 pages (2001) $14.⁹⁹

Storytelling with Rubber Stamps

Learn frugal stamping techniques to tell your stories.

Create pages that tell your family stories by using rubber stamps to make your own borders, backgrounds, embellishments, page toppers, frames and more.

Stamps make it easy to create supporting elements. Learn tips for affordable stamping—see how to use common household items like a pencil eraser as a stamp!

ISBN: 0-930500-03-3
80 pages (2001) $14.⁹⁹

One Minute Journaling

Save the tales! Never again lose an important family story.

Learn how to capture stories as they're happening, using one-minute journaling methods. You'll see how you can get your stories onto your pages in no time at all!

Available at local book, craft and scrapbook stores or by calling (800) 289-0963.

Bonus

ISBN: 0-930500-04-1
208 pages (2001) $14.⁹⁹

I'm Too Blessed to Be Depressed

From stressed to blessed in 30 days.

Lift your spirits and cheer your soul with stories that reflect life's complexity and life's joy. Collected from women of all ages and all walks of life, these stories celebrate the many choices we have—and they remind us of how fortunate we really are. It's the perfect pre-scription for the blues!

A GIFT

If you've enjoyed the guided journaling in this book, be sure to sign up at www.scrapbookstorytelling.com *for my free monthly broadcast, called Story Starters. Click the* **Free Newsletter** *button on the home page.*